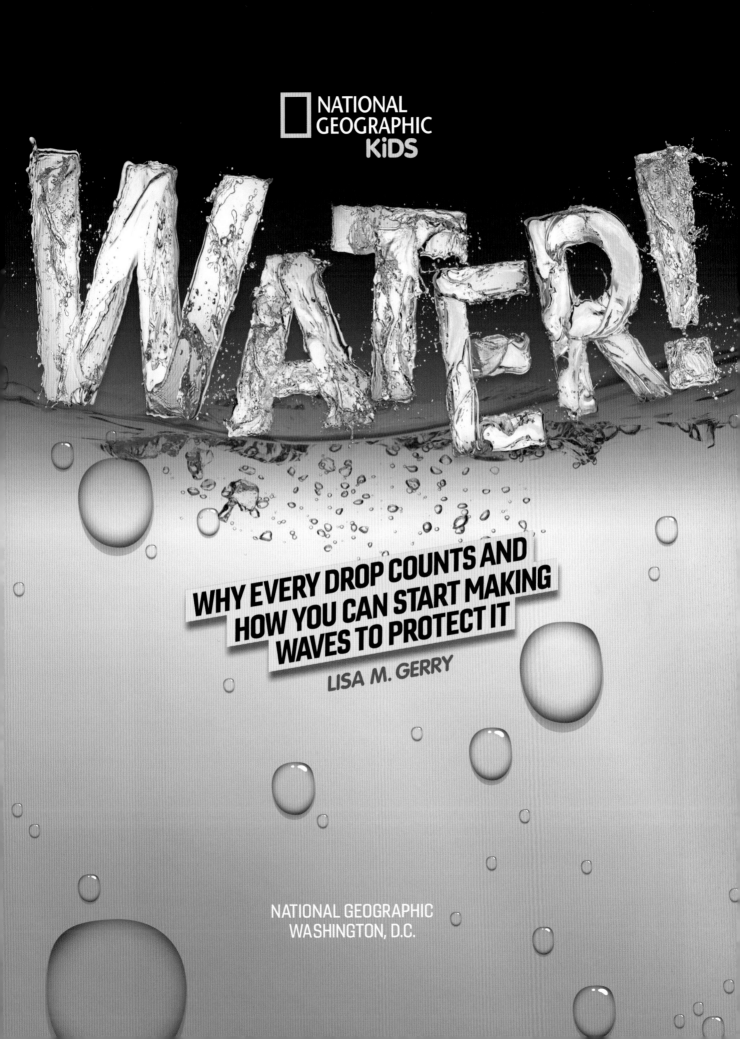

NATIONAL
GEOGRAPHIC
KiDS

# WATER!

WHY EVERY DROP COUNTS AND
HOW YOU CAN START MAKING
WAVES TO PROTECT IT

LISA M. GERRY

NATIONAL GEOGRAPHIC
WASHINGTON, D.C.

# CONTENTS

# INTRODUCTION

**W**hen I was growing up on Long Island, New York, U.S.A., all I knew about the water that flowed out of our kitchen faucet was that it was stored in the giant water tower that loomed high above our small community. Later I learned that the actual source of our water was an underground formation called an aquifer. Big pumps brought water to the surface to be distributed to our homes and stored in that high tower. I also learned that how our community used the land could affect the quality of that groundwater—our drinking water—and therefore our health.

I have been fascinated by Earth's water cycle ever since. We live on a remarkably blue planet, but most of that blue is ocean water—too salty to drink or use to grow crops. Less than one percent of Earth's water is fresh and easily accessible to us. And that water is finite, but of course the demands of the global population are not.

Everything we use, wear, buy, and eat takes water to make—sometimes a surprisingly large amount. Making a simple cotton shirt can take up to 700 gallons (2,650 L)! That's mostly because cotton plants require a lot of water to grow. When we add up the water to produce our food, clothes, computers, electricity, and everything else, it takes about 2,000 gallons (7,571 L) a day to keep the average American's lifestyle afloat!

The good news is there's so much we can do to conserve water, become more conscious consumers, and generally live happy, healthy lives while using less water.

Once we shrink our water footprint, we can share more water with the natural world. It's water that makes the planet so beautiful and rich in biodiversity—the birds, bees, fish, and trees that we enjoy and benefit from every day. But nature is in trouble. Many rivers and streams are running dry, wetlands are disappearing, and pollution is flowing through rivers and streams to lakes and coastal bays.

For these reasons and more, freshwater life is suffering. According to one study, since 1970 the world's population of freshwater vertebrates has declined by 84 percent. Think about that! For every 100 frogs and fish that were around 50 years ago, there are now only 16. That is a dramatic loss of life. And we are part of this beautiful web of life. We're all in this together.

We can choose to write a new water story. We can conserve water and add flow back to rivers. We can ask our government officials and engineers to manage dams a bit differently. Even as they continue to provide us with flood control, hydroelectric power, and water storage, dams can be operated in a way that restores some of the flows and habitats fish and birds need to survive. We can reduce the pollutants running off farmlands and urban streets that pose risks to people and nature alike.

Remember, water connects us to all living beings across space and time. Some of the water you drink today might have quenched a dinosaur's thirst. Water is finite, and it cycles endlessly.

Water is life.

So dive into this wonderful book! You will get many ideas on how you can become a Water Warrior. Share what you learn with your family, friends, and neighbors. Nature needs your creativity, energy, and compassion. After all, if we don't speak and act for the rivers and fish, who will?

**Sandra Postel**
National Geographic Explorer
Stockholm Water Prize Laureate 2021

Pukang waterfall, Thailand

# WATER 101

>> **EARTH'S WATER IS ONE OF OUR PLANET'S CROWN JEWELS.** Imagine you are an astronaut floating in space. As you take in your surroundings, you look back at where you came from—at your home planet, Earth.

What do you think would most stand out?

It likely wouldn't be that Earth is full of life, or even that it has an impressive atmosphere. What would probably make your jaw drop is all that beautiful blue water.

Of all the planets and moons in our solar system, only Earth has large, stable bodies of water on its surface. Earth is known as "the water planet."

But even with water as far as the eye can see, Earth is experiencing some big-time water woes—some major environmental issues we will all need to face head-on and work together to resolve.

To learn more about the ins and outs of our water world—and how you can become a Water Warrior to protect our planet and one of its most precious resources—read on!

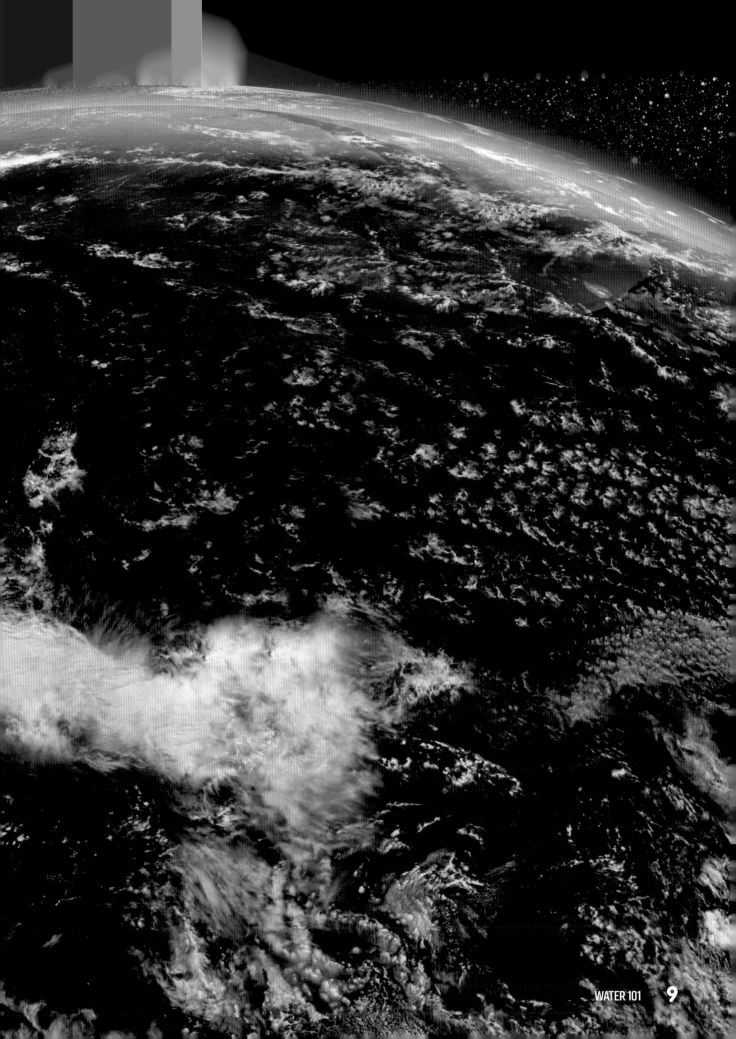

# Water Issues
# ARE MORE IMPORTANT THAN EVER.

» **IF YOU LIVE SOMEWHERE WHERE WATER IS PLENTIFUL AND CLEAN, YOU MIGHT BE THINKING TO YOURSELF, *EARTH HAS A WATER PROBLEM? I HAD NO IDEA!***

So let's back up: Even if you don't yet know the water challenges Earth is facing (and all the ways you can help), you still probably know that water is *really* important.

For starters, just as we need air to breathe and food to eat, humans need water to live.

Beyond that, water is part of practically every process in our day-to-day lives. We use water to grow our food, create electricity, make our clothes, clean our food and bodies—and so much more.

But the thing is ...
- Not everyone on Earth has enough water.
- Some people don't have access to clean, safe water.
- And, as the effects of climate change increase, so do many of the dangerous disruptions to Earth's water cycle.

So the time is now to learn about water, why water issues are so very important, and how you can be a part of making a positive impact on our planet.

Stormwater is water from rain or snow that accumulates on Earth's surface—like puddles!

ABOUT **60** PERCENT OF THE ADULT HUMAN BODY IS **WATER.**

# 6 REASONS WE SHOULD ALL CARE ABOUT WATER

The world's water NEEDS OUR ATTENTION. Here are just SIX OF THE MANY REASONS WHY.

**1 Humans need water to live.** We depend on having freshwater for our survival, as do the plants and animals around the world. When the amount of water we have access to decreases, it impacts many important parts of our lives, including sanitation, food production, energy, manufacturing, and issues of equality.

**2 ALL species on Earth need water to live.** Every living thing on Earth, from the smallest microorganisms to a 200-ton (181-t) blue whale, needs water to survive. And many factors—including the ways humans have affected the natural water cycle—have put freshwater plants and animals in danger. In fact, freshwater species are going extinct faster than land or vertebrate sea species. In just 50 years, the total number of freshwater vertebrates, such as fish, turtles, and otters, has dropped by an estimated 84 percent!

IN 2021, **HARMFUL ALGAL BLOOMS,** CAUSED BY HUMAN BEHAVIOR, **KILLED** THE **SEAGRASS** FLORIDA MANATEES EAT AND NEED TO SURVIVE.

**3** **Many people don't have the water they need.** Despite living on a water planet, an estimated 1.4 billion people on Earth live in areas where they are at risk of not having enough clean freshwater to meet their needs. This could be due to a lack of water in the region or a lack of treatment and delivery systems. And, even as the world's population increases, the amount of water does not. The same water has existed on this planet for most of its 4.5 billion years, and it continues to move around Earth in a natural water cycle. As the population increases, the *demand* for water grows, but the *supply* does not.

RESEARCHERS CALCULATED THAT MORE THAN HALF OF ALL **SEA TURTLES** MAY HAVE INGESTED **PLASTIC.**

**4** **Many of Earth's bodies of water are polluted.** Water pollution occurs when bodies of water—lakes, oceans, and rivers—become contaminated as a result of human activities. A powerful example of this is the plastic pollution in the world's oceans. It is estimated that by the year 2050 there will be more plastic in the oceans than fish, by weight. And this plastic pollution is very harmful. It hurts sea creatures that get tangled up in it or accidentally eat it. And, when humans eat fish that have eaten plastic, they ingest tiny bits of plastic, too.

**5** **The quality of many people's drinking water is poor:** For many, many people around the world, the only water that they have access to isn't healthy to drink. But for some, there is no other option. For example, some drinking water contains bacteria, chemicals such as bleach, heavy metals such as lead, viruses, and even radioactive contaminants.

**6** **As climate change worsens, water issues do, too!** As Earth continues to warm, and as weather patterns change as a result of climate change, the natural water cycle is disrupted in many ways. As a result, glaciers are melting, the temperature of the ocean is rising (which makes it harder for some sea creatures to live and thrive), and some parts of the world have more severe droughts, while others have more severe floods.

*BUT THERE IS GOOD NEWS, AND THE GOOD NEWS IS YOU!*
# YES, YOU!

The first step to addressing the world's water worries is to learn about the challenges Earth is facing.

Then you can start to understand how your actions and behaviors play a role. And you can commit to becoming a WATER WARRIOR!

So let's start from the beginning ... the very beginning.

## WHERE DID EARTH'S WATER COME FROM?

When Earth formed, more than 4.5 billion years ago, it came together sort of like a snowball, growing and collecting matter bit by bit. But instead of snow, it was made from cosmic dust that had been created when various planets and asteroids crashed into each other. As Earth began to take shape, a ring of water vapor formed around it.

Earth was incredibly hot—too hot for the water vapor to condense from a gas into a liquid and fall from the atmosphere onto the new planet's surface. But then, about 700 million years later, Earth cooled to below 212°F (100°C). The water vapor condensed and fell as rain, and it continued to fall for centuries—filling up all of the basins on Earth and creating our oceans. Since then, relatively tiny amounts of water have also arrived on Earth via comets, which are like cosmic snowballs or icy balls of gas.

# WHERE ON EARTH IS ALL THE WATER TODAY?

>> **W**ater is *everywhere*. And not just in the oceans and lakes. Water is in the plants and trees, in the soil, in the air—water is even in you. Most of the water on Earth, though—about 97.5 percent—is salt water, mainly found in the oceans. Only about 2.5 percent of the water on our planet is freshwater. The majority of Earth's freshwater exists in the form of glaciers and ice caps, with only 1.2 percent found on Earth's surface (rivers, ponds, groundwater aquifers, lakes, and wetlands), which is where we get most of the freshwater we use for our many needs (including drinking, bathing, and watering crops).

**97.5% OF ALL WATER ON EARTH IS SALT WATER!
THAT MEANS ONLY 2.5% IS FRESHWATER.**

SALT WATER: 97.5%

**OF THE 2.5% THAT IS FRESHWATER,
HERE'S THE BREAKDOWN:**

GLACIERS AND ICE CAPS: 68.7%

GROUNDWATER: 30.1%

RIVERS, LAKES, AND OTHER
SURFACE FRESHWATER: 1.2%

# WATER...
## THE SHAPE-SHIFTER!

**W**ater moves around the planet as part of the natural water cycle. Some water stays on land for a long time, while some moves from land to air rather quickly. Water that is stored in ice caps or as groundwater deep below Earth's surface can stay there for thousands of years, while water in oceans and lakes might remain for just days or weeks before it begins to evaporate into the atmosphere.

Check out eight of the many forms this shape-shifting substance can take on Earth.

### ≪ GLACIER

Glaciers are large, thickened ice masses made up of fallen snow that has compressed over many years. A glacier forms when snow does not melt for many years and slowly turns to ice. Glaciers cover about 10 percent of the total land area on Earth, and most of the world's glaciers are found in Antarctica and Greenland. The largest glacier on Earth, the Lambert-Fisher Glacier in Antarctica, is 250 miles (400 km) long and up to 60 miles (100 km) wide.

### ≪ OCEAN

The ocean is a continuous body of salt water that covers more than 70 percent of Earth's surface. Geographers have divided the ocean into five different areas: the Pacific, Atlantic, Indian, Arctic, and Southern. The ocean is the world's largest habitat, and it is estimated that only 5 percent of it has been explored.

### ≪ GROUNDWATER

Just as water fills a sponge, water that falls as rain and then seeps belowground fills the holes and pores of rocky materials such as sand, gravel, and porous sandstone. These belowground structures that hold or transmit water are called aquifers.

AN **ICE SHEET** IS A DOME-SHAPED PIECE OF GLACIER ICE THAT COVERS MORE THAN 12 MILLION ACRES (50,000 SQ KM).

## ≫ SEA ICE

Sea ice is frozen ocean water that floats on the surface. Unlike glaciers, which form on land, sea ice freezes in the oceans in the Arctic and Antarctic regions, near the North and South Poles. The salt lowers the water's freezing point, which means salt water needs to be colder than freshwater to freeze. There is sea ice all year-round, but the amount of sea ice increases during the winter months and shrinks during summer.

## ≫ RIVERS

A river is a large natural stream of flowing water. Rivers begin at headwaters, or a source (such as a lake, or melting snow or glacier ice), then flow downhill as a stream, collecting groundwater and precipitation. Other smaller streams, called tributaries, can also contribute to a river. The river continues to flow until it reaches its mouth, or outlet, which is where it empties into a larger body of water, such as a lake or ocean.

## ≫ SEAS

Seas are part of the ocean, but they're on the border—usually where ocean and land meet—and they're partially enclosed by land. The famous Dead Sea is actually a super salty landlocked lake bordered by Israel, Jordan, and the West Bank. It has the lowest elevation of any body of water on the surface of Earth.

## ≫ ICEBERG

Usually found in the Arctic, North Atlantic, and Southern Oceans, an iceberg is made of freshwater and is a large piece of ice that has broken off a glacier or an ice shelf and floated away. Icebergs are classified by size. From smallest to largest they're called growlers, bergy bits, small berg, medium berg, large berg, and very large berg (meaning more than 240 feet [73 m] high and more than 670 feet [204 m] long!).

## ≫ LAKES

Lakes are bodies of water that are surrounded by land. They are mostly freshwater and are formed from rain, snow, melting ice, streams, and groundwater seepage. The five lakes (Huron, Ontario, Michigan, Erie, and Superior) that make up the Great Lakes (located between the United States and Canada), hold 21 percent of the world's liquid surface freshwater.

# Water on the Move:
# THE WATER CYCLE
# EXPLAINED

**E**arth contains a finite amount of water, and it is constantly moving in, on, and above the planet in a natural water cycle. This rotation of water is necessary for the survival of all the living things on Earth, and it connects us to one another. The water we drink today could be the same water that cycled through a dinosaur, erupted as steam from a volcano, was used to make George Washington's coffee, or was bathed in by an ancient Neanderthal!

## SUN HEATS WATER
The sun heats the water on Earth's surface, causing it to evaporate from places like oceans, rivers, and lakes. Water molecules then rise as vapor into the atmosphere.

## TRANSPIRATION
Water also rises into the atmosphere through transpiration. Water from the soil is absorbed by plants and trees through their roots, then travels up to the leaves and evaporates, returning to the atmosphere.

## CONDENSATION

Once it is in the atmosphere, the water vapor cools and, with the help of condensation nuclei, condenses into clouds. For a water molecule to condense, it needs to find a particle that has a radius of at least 1/250,000 of an inch (one millionth of a meter) to bond to. These teeny-tiny particles are called condensation nuclei and might be specks of dirt, dust, or salt (from the ocean, for example). This means that every cloud droplet has a little something extra at its core—things like smoke particles from a volcano or fire, windblown dirt, or a bit of salt from sea spray.

## PRECIPITATION

Carried on air currents, clouds move all around the world. They grow and sometimes combine with other clouds. At a certain point, they become too full and the water falls as rain, hail, sleet, or snow, which is known as precipitation.

## GROUNDWATER

If water falls back down to cold parts of Earth's surface, it may freeze and accumulate as ice caps and glaciers. If it falls on warm areas of Earth, it flows back into bodies of water (thanks to gravity!), or soaks into the ground and becomes groundwater.

# FRESHWATER SPECIES NEED OUR HELP!

**W**hen humans interfere in Earth's natural water cycle, there are often unintended—and harmful—consequences. That's one of the reasons why freshwater habitats—and the animals that depend on these habitats to survive—are in trouble. In fact, freshwater species are going extinct faster than vertebrate species that live on land or in the oceans.

Because all life on the planet is connected, when one part of the web is hurting, every other part is affected.

Here are some of the main ways freshwater ecosystems are being harmed:

## ⌄CLIMATE CHANGE

Humans' actions are causing Earth's climate patterns to change, which is having a big impact on weather, oceans and other bodies of water, plants, and animals. For more on the effects of climate change and what you can do to help, see chapter 5.

## ⌃TAKING TOO MUCH

All around the world certain species are being threatened by humans taking so much, so fast that nature can't keep up by reproducing or replenishing its supply. Two examples of this are overfishing (which includes fish caught to eat as well as fish accidentally caught by large fishing boats) and extracting too much water from lakes, aquifers, and rivers for human use (such as drinking and farming).

## «INVASIVE SPECIES

When a species that does not naturally occur in a particular environment begins living there, it can cause major problems. Invasive species can take resources from species that already live there, spread diseases, destroy habitats, and more. Many invasive species are introduced to new ecosystems by humans, some by accident (such as when organisms like crabs or algae hitch a ride on the hull of a ship), or on purpose (such as when exotic pets are released into the wild by their owners).

## «DAMS

Dams are structures built (by humans and some animals, such as beavers) to hold back water in a river or stream. When humans build a dam, it creates a lake-like body of water called a reservoir. People can use the water in the reservoir to generate hydroelectric power, for needs like farming or drinking, or even for fun activities such as boating or swimming. Dams are also sometimes built to help prevent rivers from flooding. But dams can create a whole host of environmental problems by preventing fish such as salmon from reaching spawning grounds, interrupting the natural water flow to downstream coastal estuaries (where a freshwater river or stream meets the ocean), and eliminating habitats for species that require flowing water to live.

## «HURTING HABITATS

When humans pollute or remove a habitat, they put the wildlife living there in danger. For example, when humans fill in wetlands and cover them over to build houses or roads, and when we pollute natural bodies of water with plastic, chemicals, or farm runoff, we endanger the wildlife that inhabits these places.

## A CLOSER LOOK AT DAMS

Dams can have an impact on water flow, temperature, depth, and more, potentially harming some wildlife that live both upstream and downstream. Take salmon, for example. Salmon are big-time travelers. They are born in freshwater, swim far out to sea to get bigger and more mature, and then they return to where they were born to spawn, or reproduce. The creation of dams, however, has blocked many salmon, preventing them from migrating. It has also made it challenging, and sometimes impossible, for salmon to reproduce. And this is just one example! Many other creatures are affected when dams disrupt the natural flow of rivers.

When the natural water cycle is interrupted, the effects trickle down ... so much so that even the dirt is disrupted! By blocking rivers from flowing, dams also prevent sediment, little bits of sand and rocks, from traveling downstream to be deposited where it's needed on shorelines or in bodies of water (where it might serve as a sandbar ideally suited for wading birds and mollusks).

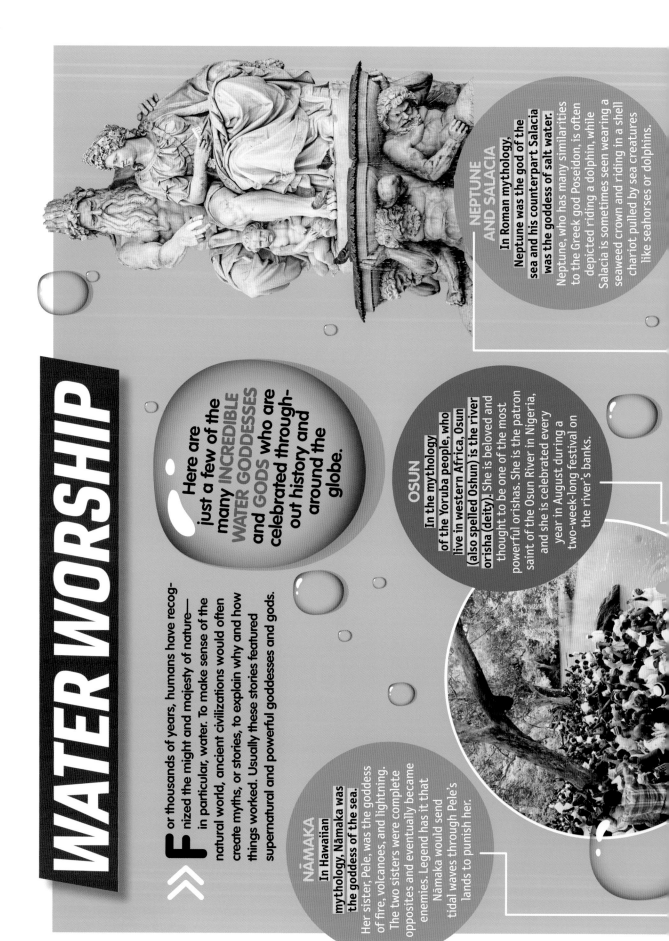

# WATER WORSHIP

**F**or thousands of years, humans have recognized the might and majesty of nature—in particular, water. To make sense of the natural world, ancient civilizations would often create myths, or stories, to explain why and how things worked. Usually these stories featured supernatural and powerful goddesses and gods.

Here are just a few of the many INCREDIBLE WATER GODDESSES and GODS who are celebrated throughout history and around the globe.

## NEPTUNE AND SALACIA

In Roman mythology, Neptune was the god of the sea and his counterpart Salacia was the goddess of salt water. Neptune, who has many similarities to the Greek god Poseidon, is often depicted riding a dolphin, while Salacia is sometimes seen wearing a seaweed crown and riding in a shell chariot pulled by sea creatures like seahorses or dolphins.

## OSUN

In the mythology of the Yoruba people, who live in western Africa, Osun (also spelled Oshun) is the river orisha (deity). She is beloved and thought to be one of the most powerful orishas. She is the patron saint of the Osun River in Nigeria, and she is celebrated every year in August during a two-week-long festival on the river's banks.

## NĀMAKA

In Hawaiian mythology, Nāmaka was the goddess of the sea. Her sister, Pele, was the goddess of fire, volcanoes, and lightning. The two sisters were complete opposites and eventually became enemies. Legend has it that Nāmaka would send tidal waves through Pele's lands to punish her.

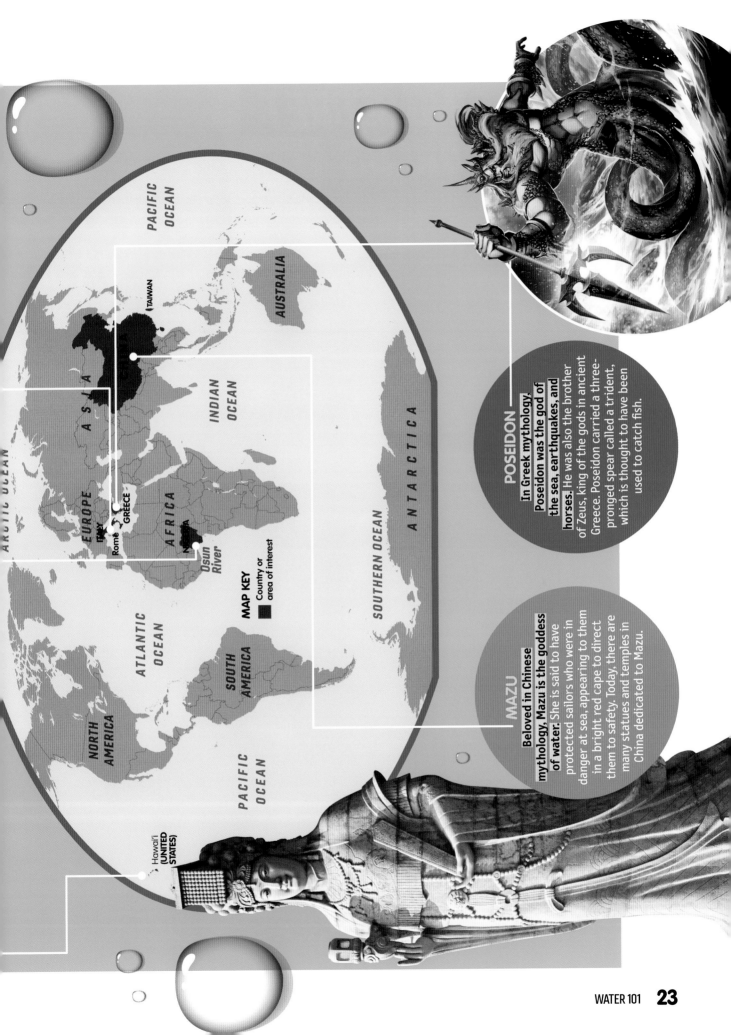

PACIFIC OCEAN

ARCTIC OCEAN

EUROPE

ASIA

AFRICA

INDIAN OCEAN

AUSTRALIA

TAIWAN

GREECE

ITALY

Rome

NIGERIA

Osun River

ATLANTIC OCEAN

NORTH AMERICA

SOUTH AMERICA

PACIFIC OCEAN

Hawai'i (UNITED STATES)

SOUTHERN OCEAN

ANTARCTICA

**MAP KEY**
■ Country or area of interest

### POSEIDON

In Greek mythology, Poseidon was the god of the sea, earthquakes, and horses. He was also the brother of Zeus, king of the gods in ancient Greece. Poseidon carried a three-pronged spear called a trident, which is thought to have been used to catch fish.

### MAZU

Beloved in Chinese mythology, Mazu is the goddess of water. She is said to have protected sailors who were in danger at sea, appearing to them in a bright red cape to direct them to safety. Today, there are many statues and temples in China dedicated to Mazu.

# SHARING SECRET WATER WORLDS

## Q & A With Jenny Adler

The Floridan aquifer stretches for more than 100,000 square miles (259,000 sq km) of the United States. It lies below all of Florida and parts of Alabama, Georgia, and South Carolina.

**N**ational Geographic Explorer Jenny Adler began her career as a marine biologist, studying the many organisms—both big and small—that live in the sea. But Jenny soon realized she wanted to do more than study the natural world; she wanted to share it and show it to people. She figured if she could communicate how cool these ecosystems are, people would begin to care about them and want to protect them!

So that's exactly what Jenny does. She uses her passion for underwater photography to introduce people to water worlds they might otherwise never see. One of these worlds is the Floridan aquifer.

The Floridan aquifer is a system of underground rock that is porous, meaning it has holes that water or air can pass through. As water trickles down from Earth's surface, it is held underground in the limestone. The water in this rock, from tiny holes to huge passageways, make up the aquifer.

And Jenny does something super special: She scuba dives and takes photos inside the aquifer's underwater caves.

**Q: How do you get into the aquifer?**
Florida's springs are like a bowl of clear freshwater. Then, somewhere in a spring—usually at the bottom or the side—there will be this black hole. That's the spring vent and that's where the water flows up from the aquifer. It's kind of like this opening to this underground labyrinth of caves, which is pretty cool.

**Q: What inspired you to swim through that little hole and scuba dive in the aquifer?**
Springs are really beautiful to swim in and I was swimming in them in all my spare time. I was learning so much about them and the curiosity was killing me. I thought, *there are openings at the bottom of all these springs—I want to know what's in there, and I want to see what's it's like.*

**Q: So first you needed to become a certified cave diver and then you ventured into the aquifer. What is it like inside an aquifer?**
People always think that aquifers are really colorful and bright because in the photos there might be 10 or 15 lights lighting them up. But in reality, in the aquifers, it's the most pitch-dark place you could ever imagine. It's like going into a closet, shutting the door, and putting a blanket over your head. There are no stars, there's no moon, there's no light sneaking in from anywhere—it's absolutely, completely dark. So, when you're in there, you really start to focus on other things, like the sound of the bubbles from your regulator.

**Q: What do you love about cave diving?**
When I'm diving, I'm completely hyper-focused on what I'm doing, and my body and my mind are relaxed. I feel distracted above water sometimes, but underwater, it's very peaceful. You feel completely weightless, and the water is so clear that you almost can't really tell that you're in the water, so it feels like you're hovering in outer space. It's an amazing feeling.

**Q: What surprised you about the aquifer?**
The caves really vary in size. At one spot, you might have to squeeze through an area where you don't think you're going to fit, and then the cave will open up into a room that's big enough to fit a Boeing 747. The caves will go from being huge to tiny and from rock that's full of holes like Swiss cheese to rock that's really smooth. As I experienced so many different parts of it, I started to understand how complex the world is beneath our feet. It's really rewarding and also sort of mind-blowing.

**Q: Are there fish and other living things in there?**
In the springs there is a ton of life, but once you enter the caves where it's dark, there isn't much that can survive there. But there are these cool cave crayfish and amphipods that live in the caves. Most of them are albino; they're completely white, and they've adapted to live in the cave.

**Q: How did swimming through the aquifer affect the way you think about how you use water?**
It made me realize how close we are to our water, and how crucial it is that we protect it. What we do at the surface has a huge impact on the water beneath our feet.

Some 90 percent of people who live in Florida get their drinking water from groundwater, including water that comes from the Floridan aquifer.

# H2-Oh-Wow!

**Check out this WEIRD BUT TRUE Water Wonder.**

**Spotted Lake,** BRITISH COLUMBIA, CANADA

Each summer, the water evaporates out of this lake, leaving dazzling pools in various bright colors. The colors vary depending on the mineral deposits in each particular spot. The lake is said to have special healing powers, and over the years minerals from it have been collected to make everything from World War I ammunition to modern-day spa treatments.

# CHAPTER 2

# WATER AND YOU

>> **WHAT DO THE CLOTHES ON YOUR BACK, THE FOOD ON YOUR PLATE, THE TRANSPORTATION YOU TAKE, AND THE PAPER IN YOUR NOTEBOOK ALL HAVE IN COMMON?**

For starters, they all require water to create!

It's easy to understand just how valuable water is when you're really thirsty and you chug down a cool, refreshing glass of it. But we need water for way more than just drinking. You might be surprised by just how much water is used in almost every product and process we encounter in our day-to-day lives.

Some communities have all the water they need (and sometimes more than they need); others are desperately struggling just to get enough.

Read on to find out all the different ways that water is used around the world and in our daily lives.

# HOW MUCH WATER DOES IT TAKE TO MAKE...?

>> **E**verything we eat, everything we buy, everything we wear—water is used in some way to make it all. And some things use *a lot* of water. How much water something uses is called its "water footprint." And everything and everyone has one.

Take, for example, a cheese pizza. To make the mozzarella cheese for one pizza, it takes about 165 gallons (625 L) of water. To make the wheat flour for the crust requires about 145 gallons (549 L) of water. The tomato sauce? About 20 gallons (76 L) of water. Adding all its components together, one cheese pizza has a water footprint of about 330 gallons (1,249 L) of water.

By not wasting food, buying secondhand clothes and toys, and reusing old items, you're not only conserving the specific materials that make up those items—like grain, cotton, plastic, and wood—you're also saving water!

**JEANS**
(1 pair):
About
**2,000**
GALLONS
(7,571 L)

**COTTON T-SHIRT:**
About
**700**
GALLONS
(2,650 L)

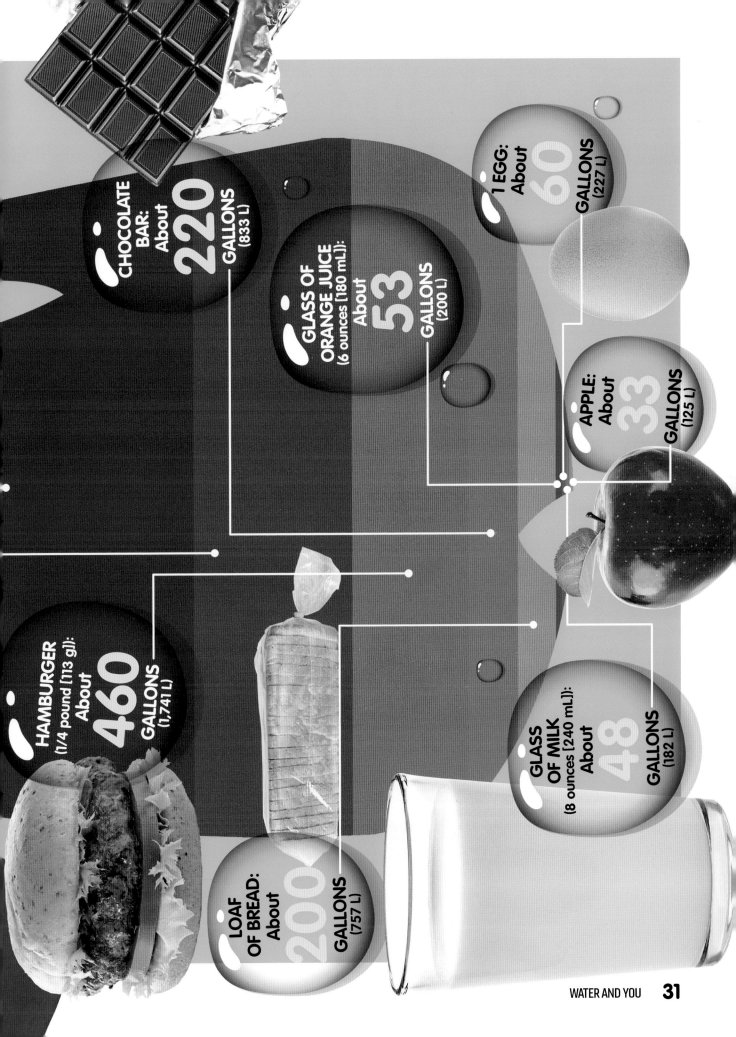

**CHOCOLATE BAR:** About **220** GALLONS (833 L)

**GLASS OF ORANGE JUICE** (6 ounces [180 mL]): About **53** GALLONS (200 L)

**1 EGG:** About **60** GALLONS (227 L)

**APPLE:** About **33** GALLONS (125 L)

**HAMBURGER** (1/4 pound [113 g]): About **460** GALLONS (1,741 L)

**LOAF OF BREAD:** About **200** GALLONS (757 L)

**GLASS OF MILK** (8 ounces [240 mL]): About **48** GALLONS (182 L)

# THE MANY (MANY!) WAYS WE USE WATER

>> **H**aving enough freshwater for people to drink is very important, but freshwater is used for much more than just hydrating our bodies. Here are some of the important ways that freshwater from surface water and groundwater sources is used.

## ≫SANITATION

In many cases, when someone flushes a toilet, water carries the waste through that community's sanitary sewer system, which is typically a series of underground pipes, to a wastewater treatment facility. (For more on this process, see pp. 76–77.) While many people might not think twice about using a toilet, it is actually a life-changing—and in some cases, lifesaving—utility. About one-fourth of the world's population does not have access to basic sanitation systems, which means they have to use the bathroom without a way to safely dispose of their waste. This can lead to many serious problems, including the spread of dangerous diseases.

ABOUT **ONE-FOURTH** OF THE **WORLD'S POPULATION** DOES NOT HAVE ACCESS TO **BASIC SANITATION SYSTEMS.**

## AQUACULTURE

Aquaculture is the business of raising and harvesting organisms that live in water, such as aquatic plants called algae, and creatures such as clams, fish, and shellfish.

**AQUACULTURE IS UNDERWATER FARMING—THE BREEDING AND HARVESTING OF FISH AND AQUATIC PLANTS.**

## INDUSTRIAL USE »

Water is used to manufacture food, paper, tools, chemicals, and a whole host of other products.

## LIVESTOCK

Water is used in the raising of cows, sheep, goats, hogs, pigs, horses, and poultry.

## MINING

Water is used in mining operations, during which minerals and rocks are extracted from the earth.

## THERMOELECTRIC POWER

Thermoelectric power is the process of creating electricity with steam-driven turbine generators. Water is used to help create the steam as well as to keep these big machines cool. An estimated 195 billion gallons (738 billion L) of water are used every day to cool power equipment in the United States.

## IRRIGATION

When natural rainfall does not supply enough water to crops and grass, water from other sources is added. This is called irrigation. Water provided through irrigation helps grow crops like wheat, corn, and soybeans; plants in nurseries; and grass in places like golf courses and cemeteries, as well as the lawns of homes and businesses.

# A CLOSER LOOK:
# FROM SOURCE TO SPOUT

## Where does clean drinking water come from?

In many countries around the world, it might seem like all you have to do to get a glass of water is turn on your faucet. But by the time that freshwater reaches you wherever you are, it's already been on quite a journey.

Where exactly the water you drink comes from depends on where you live. Different countries—and even different areas within a country—get their drinking water from different sources.

In the United States, two-thirds of drinking water comes from rivers and streams, with most of the rest coming from lakes and groundwater. Groundwater is simply water that trickles down from Earth's surface through cracks and holes to places below-ground, where it can then be extracted again if needed. Sometimes this groundwater is found in a layer of underground rock. The rock acts as sort of a reservoir (or container) for the water and is called an aquifer.

Much of the drinking water in the United States travels from its original source to a water treatment plant, then to a storage tank, and finally through pipes to our homes, schools, and businesses, where we drink it, bathe in it, or wash our clothes in it.

## HOW IS WATER TREATED?

Sure, the source of your drinking water might be a lake or an underground aquifer, but that doesn't mean drinking untreated lake water or groundwater is a good—or safe—idea. It definitely isn't! There can be all sorts of contaminants and germs in these water sources that could make you sick.

So how does one get safe drinking water? In some countries, before the water reaches faucets, it goes through a treatment process at a water treatment plant. And, just as your drinking water source depends on where you live, so does the way your water gets treated.

In the United States, water goes through a multistep process before it's safe to sip. Here are some of the basic steps.

## COAGULATION AND FLOCCULATION:

Chemicals added to the water trigger a process that makes dirt and other particles bigger and heavier, so that they either settle to the bottom or are easier to filter out. These bigger, heavier particles are called floc.

## SEDIMENTATION:

During this phase, the floc settles to the bottom.

## FILTRATION:

Now that the dirt and other particles have settled to the bottom, the clear water on top is run through various filters to remove smaller particles, including parasites, bacteria, and viruses.

## DISINFECTION:

After the water has been filtered, a disinfectant is sometimes added to kill any possible remaining viruses or bacteria or to help protect from any germs that might enter the water as it's sent through pipes and into people's homes.

# DRINKING WATER AROUND THE WORLD

**D**o you know where your water comes from? It's an interesting question, because all around the country and all around the world, people get their freshwater from completely different sources. For some, all that's required to get a glass of water is to turn on the tap. For others, because there are no pipes that deliver water to their homes, they instead must use large buckets to collect water to be used and consumed throughout the day.

Here are just a few of the many FRESH-WATER SOURCES for people across the globe.

## Source: LAKES

At times during the past decade, the only sources of freshwater in Dala Township, near Yangon, Myanmar, (pictured above) were inland lakes, most of which had dried up. Residents were still able to collect water from one, but they had to wait in a long line of more than a thousand people when the government allowed access to it, once every three days. Recently, the government has made plans to begin purifying lake and well water and distributing it throughout Dala Township.

## Source: SPRINGS

About 280 people live in the Mushina Community in western Kenya, Africa, and they get their water from Shikuku Spring, a small natural accumulation of groundwater and rainwater. But the spring was becoming polluted and overgrown with algae, so an organization called the Water Project helped community members build a structure that would protect the natural spring water, making the water safer to drink.

## Source: BOTTLED WATER

In the small town of Sandbranch, Texas, U.S.A., residents don't have access to running water or a well. Instead, they use bottled water for all their drinking, bathing, and cooking needs.

## Source: WELLS

Some members of the Navajo Nation in the United States don't have running water, so they drive to water stations (pictured above) where they pay to fill large 50-gallon (190-L) jugs from a well. Some people collect water for their animals at windmills that pump water, but that water often has high levels of chemicals, making it unsafe for humans to drink.

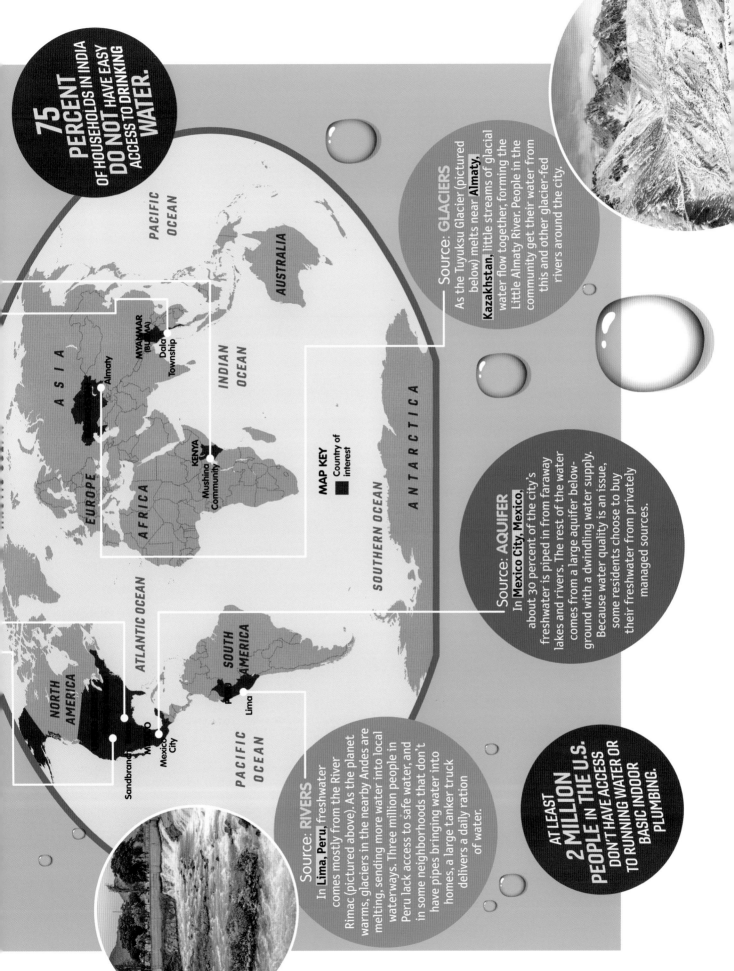

PACIFIC OCEAN

AUSTRALIA

ASIA

Almaty

MYANMAR (BURMA)

Dala Township

INDIAN OCEAN

EUROPE

AFRICA

KENYA

Mushina Community

**MAP KEY**
■ Country of interest

SOUTHERN OCEAN

ANTARCTICA

NORTH AMERICA

ATLANTIC OCEAN

SOUTH AMERICA

Sandbranch

MEXICO

Mexico City

Lima

PACIFIC OCEAN

### Source: GLACIERS

As the Tuyuksu Glacier (pictured below) melts near **Almaty, Kazakhstan**, little streams of glacial water flow together, forming the Little Almaty River. People in the community get their water from this and other glacier-fed rivers around the city.

### Source: AQUIFER

In **Mexico City, Mexico,** about 30 percent of the city's freshwater is piped in from faraway lakes and rivers. The rest of the water comes from a large aquifer below-ground with a dwindling water supply. Because water quality is an issue, some residents choose to buy their freshwater from privately managed sources.

### Source: RIVERS

In **Lima, Peru,** freshwater comes mostly from the River Rímac (pictured above). As the planet warms, glaciers in the nearby Andes are melting, sending more water into local waterways. Three million people in Peru lack access to safe water, and in some neighborhoods that don't have pipes bringing water into homes, a large tanker truck delivers a daily ration of water.

# HOW MUCH WATER DOES YOUR MORNING BATHROOM ROUTINE USE?

Do you leave the water on while you wash your face?

If **YES**, add 3 gallons (11 L) (for a newer faucet—older ones use more!).

If **NO**, add 0.5 gallon (1.9 L) (for about 30 seconds to wet and rinse your face).

Do you leave the water on while you brush your teeth?

If **YES**, add 3 gallons (11 L).

If **NO**, add 0.5 gallon (1.9 L) (for about 30 seconds to wet and rinse your toothbrush).

IN HOMES IN THE UNITED STATES, **18 GALLONS (68 L) OF WATER** IS WASTED ON AVERAGE EACH DAY DUE TO LEAKS.

Do you take a shower or bath?

**BATH** = About 70 gallons (265 L) to fill a large bathtub, and about 40 gallons (151 L) for smaller tubs

**SHOWER** = 10 to 25 gallons (38 to 95 L) every 5 minutes

THE AVERAGE AMERICAN USES ABOUT **82 GALLONS (310 L) OF WATER** PER DAY IN THEIR HOME. THAT'S EQUAL TO 1,312 EIGHT-OUNCE (240 ML) **GLASSES OF WATER!**

How many times do you flush the toilet before you head off to school?

Each flush uses 1.5 to 6 gallons (6 to 23 L) (older toilets use more water).

# 10

## WAYS TO CONSERVE WATER AT HOME

**1** Turn off the faucet when brushing your teeth or washing your face. The sink faucet flows at about one gallon (3.8 L) of water per minute. Turning it off is a super simple way to save!

**2** Eat more vegetables and go meatless one day a week. A lot of water is used to raise and feed farm animals. To produce one pound (0.5 kg) of hamburger meat, an estimated 1,840 gallons (6,965 L) of water are used.

**3** Take a shower instead of a bath. A quick shower uses less water than a full tub.

**4** Try not to waste food. Only put on your plate as much as you know you'll eat, then save the rest for leftovers. Seventy percent of all freshwater is used for agriculture, including the growing and harvesting of food.

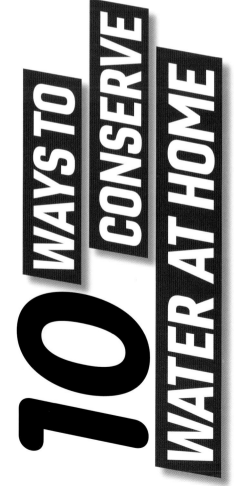

**7**

Buy less new stuff! Almost every item uses quite a bit of water to produce and ship.

**10**

Recycle! Each time a new item is created, it uses lots of water (including the harvesting of the raw materials, and the energy and electricity required to create the product). So by recycling, you can reduce the number of brand-new products that need to be made from raw materials.

**6**

Turn off lights when you leave a room, turn off electronics when they are not in use, and do whatever else you can to save energy. It takes water to produce energy, and energy to provide water. Cut down on one and you conserve both!

**9**

Use fewer single-use items, since they all require water to create. In fact, it takes at least twice as much water to produce a plastic water bottle as the amount of water inside the bottle.

**8**

Donate your old items. They won't go to the landfill and people won't need to buy new items, which use water to manufacture.

**5**

If you need to water your lawn, do it in the morning or at night when it's cooler. You'll lose less to evaporation.

THE AVERAGE AMERICAN THROWS AWAY ABOUT 80 POUNDS (36 KG) OF CLOTHING EACH YEAR.

DONATION

# WATER WARRIORS
# INVENTING NEW WAYS TO CONSERVE

## Q & A With Calden Gounden and Kairan Chetty

The Stockholm Junior Water Prize is a prestigious youth award for a water-related science project. In 2019, Calden Gounden, 18, and Kairan Chetty, 18, were finalists in the competition. The teens traveled from their homes in South Africa to Sweden to demonstrate the water-saving device they invented together, the Hydro Conservator.

At their school, part of the day is devoted to "guidance lessons," a time when students can have informal discussions with their teachers. During one of these chats, Calden and Kairan's teacher, Mr. Denli, brought up how water was becoming a scarce resource for many people and the importance of water conservation.

This got Kairan and Calden thinking. One morning, Calden noticed how much water flowed from the faucet while he was brushing his teeth. Similarly, as Kairan waited for the water in his shower to turn from cold to hot, he watched as the wasted water flowed down the drain.

They decided to put their heads together and work as a team to invent a device that would help reduce wasted water from bathroom showers and sinks.

The first part of the device is a three-way shower valve that conserves the cool water that would normally be wasted while someone waits for the water to get warm. This water is then heated, after which a valve opens, allowing it to flow out. The second part of the Hydro Conservator is a more affordable version of an automatic faucet that dispenses water only when your hand or toothbrush is underneath it.

"The automated tap has a sensor to reduce the amount of water wasted," Calden says, "as often people leave the tap open whilst brushing their teeth, just like I did. Although there are automatic taps in use, they can be quite expensive, and we got it to be more cost effective by exploring cheaper parts."

Here Calden and Kairan talk more about why water conservation is so important—and their plans for changing the world.

The Stockholm Junior Water Prize is an international competition for high school students to present their water-research projects.

**Q: How did you develop the technology that you used for the Hydro Conservator?**

**Kairan:** Once we fully identified what we wanted to achieve, it was a matter of finding the simplest combination of computer/microcontroller and electronic valves to build the prototype. We had much heartache and many setbacks. In fact, we blew up two Raspberry Pi's [a single-board computer], which actually worked in our favor, as we settled on a more cost-effective microcontroller. Then we had to develop the code to make everything work smoothly and control the relays to switch stuff off and on at the right times. We learned so much about what it takes to be an inventor.

**Q: Why do you think it is important for people to conserve water?**

**Kairan:** If we continue to waste and pollute the water we have, first, it will become scarce and expensive. Next, it will create conflict as each country tries to secure water for its citizens. This is not something we can leave for tomorrow; it is something we need to do right now. We did a brief assessment of the Hydro Conservator and found it has the potential to conserve more than 16 billion liters

[4 billion gallons] of water per day in households that employ taps and showers throughout the world.

**Q: What did you learn about yourselves and about water conservation during the process of creating the Hydro Conservator?**

**Calden:** I have learned that if you put your mind to something, you can really create something amazing and also that hard work does pay off. I also learned that I am resilient and have the ability to make a difference. I learned that we need to collaborate across the world to share ideas and gain more insight into what we can do to conserve water—we are not alone. And I have learned that across the world, people waste large amounts of water and there is a lack of conservation and awareness, which is depleting our current limited water supply rapidly.

**Kairan:** I am determined more than ever to make a difference. I love looking at aspects of everyday life to see how they can be improved, and I will devote whatever skills I acquire to invent things to make the world a

better place. Like every journey starts with a single step in the right direction, the Hydro Conservator for me is my first step.

**Q: What would your advice be to other young people who would like to help create solutions to some of the environmental issues facing us today?**

**Kairan:** It is important that you not leave your destiny in anyone else's hands. Do not fear failure; it is a good way to learn new things. Be inquisitive and ask questions. Pursue your ideas with real energy. Research, discuss, and build prototypes. Never be afraid to embrace differing points of view; readily collaborate to achieve success. Who knows? You may be sitting on an idea that is the next big invention, on the same scale as the wheel.

**Calden:** Look around you daily and find things you relate to, no matter where you live and your circumstances. Find problems where you come from and that will help you to find the solutions needed. No idea is silly; we all can make a difference.

# H₂-Oh-Wow!

## Check out this WEIRD BUT TRUE Water Wonder.

**The Everglades, FLORIDA, U.S.A.**

The spectacular swampy Everglades system is one of a kind. Nine different habitats have been identified here! It's one of the only places in the world where crocodiles and alligators coexist, and it's a safe haven for numerous endangered and threatened animals, including the endangered Florida panther. The Everglades are also home to the elusive ghost orchid (only about 2,000 are known to exist), and sadly, many South Florida orchids have become endangered due to overcollecting.

Much of the water in the Everglades comes from rainfall, both the rain that falls directly onto the area and rain that falls elsewhere and then flows here. When Florida receives a lot of rain, the largest lake in the state, Lake Okeechobee, overflows, sending water streaming through the Everglades wetland ecosystem.

# CHAPTER 3

# WATER, WATER EVERYWHERE...
## or Is It?

>> **IF YOU ARE SOMEONE WHO CAN GO TO THE SINK, TURN ON THE FAUCET, AND GET CLEAN FRESHWATER, YOU MIGHT THINK THAT EVERYONE IN THE WORLD HAS A SIMILARLY SEAMLESS EXPERIENCE.** But the reality is that there are many places where people don't have this opportunity.

The word "scarcity" means "shortage." Freshwater scarcity means that there is a dangerously low supply of freshwater—sometimes not enough to meet the needs of the people, crops, and animals in a community.

More than a billion people around the world experience fresh-water scarcity: Either there isn't enough water to meet the needs of the community, or there aren't dependable ways to get water from a source to people who need it. And 2.7 billion people experience water scarcity for at least one month of the year. Unfortunately, as the world's population continues to grow and climate change increasingly impacts weather and water systems, more people in more places are struggling with this issue.

This might sound grim and maybe even a little bit scary. But here's the thing: The first step toward addressing a problem and helping people who are struggling is to gather as much information as you can about the issue. Then, armed with that understanding, you can begin to find ways to be part of the solution. So—let's do it!

A young girl draws water from a well in the Thar Desert, in Rajasthan, India.

Flooding in Dhaka, Bangladesh

# What Causes
## FRESHWATER
## SCARCITY?

**THERE ARE MANY REASONS WHY SOME PEOPLE AND COMMUNITIES AROUND THE WORLD AREN'T ABLE TO ACCESS THE FRESHWATER THEY NEED.**

### ≪ CLIMATE CHANGE

Climate patterns around the world are changing. Some places are getting much more rain than in the past, which is leading to increased flooding. Other places are getting much less rain than they used to, which leads to water sources drying up and increased drought.

### POLLUTION≫

Two billion people in the world only have access to drinking water that is polluted with human waste, according to the World Health Organization. This is very dangerous as it leads to diseases like cholera, typhoid, polio, and dysentery. Another 144 million people in the world get their drinking water directly from sources on the surface of the planet, such as lakes, rivers, and ponds, without any sort of treatment. This is concerning because, more and more, surface waters are polluted by waste from big factories, sewage, and fertilizers and pesticides that flow into them from nearby lawns and farms.

### INFRASTRUCTURE

People use different methods to extract the freshwater that is beneath the ground (called groundwater). One of the most common ways is to use a pump to bring the water up to Earth's surface. In places where the governments don't have a lot of money, sometimes they are not able to build the wells or buy the pumps, or if they are, they might only be able to build very few. **This is why an estimated 206 million people in the world have to travel more than 30 minutes to obtain water from their closest drinking water source. And it's mostly women and children who do this job.**

### POPULATION INCREASE AND WATER WASTE

As the world's population increases, more people are using water, so there is less to go around. And in many places in the world, a tremendous amount of water is wasted. For example, every day in the United States, an estimated six billion gallons (22.7 billion L) of treated water are lost due to leaky pipes.

# DAY ZERO

**WHAT IS DAY ZERO? IN LATE 2017, GOVERNMENT OFFICIALS IN THE CITY OF CAPE TOWN, SOUTH AFRICA, ISSUED AN ALARMING WARNING.** The city's water supply was almost gone, and they predicted that in the next year they would have to turn off all the water. They named the day they thought this was going to happen "Day Zero." Government officials told the more than four million people who lived in the city that water would no longer flow from the faucets in their homes. Instead, people would need to go to a collection point nearby and get a water ration, or a certain amount to use throughout the day.

**Why did it happen?** Most of the freshwater that people use in Cape Town and that flows through the city's pipes comes from six dams that collect rainwater. The problem was that Cape Town had been experiencing a drought, or lack of rain that leads to very dry conditions, for more than three years. So, the reservoirs were beginning to go dry.

**What happened in the end?** The people of Cape Town came together and made a huge effort to use less water. They were allowed to use only a certain amount each day, by law. They collected water from their showers to use again, they didn't flush the toilet after every use, and they collected rainwater to use in their swimming pools. The government even created public maps that showed which houses in each neighborhood were doing a good job conserving water. Then rains came and began refilling the dams. In the end, Cape Town was able to prevent Day Zero from happening.

## TWO-MINUTE SHOWER TUNES

When the drought in Cape Town was at its worst, to conserve water, the government asked its citizens to keep their showers to two minutes or less. A local communications agency came up with a chart-topping idea. They asked some of the best South African musicians to record two-minute versions of their biggest hits. Next, they created a "2-Minute Shower Songs" playlist so that people could play (or sing!) one of the songs, being careful to turn off the water before the last note was sung.

**THIS AREA HAS LIMITED WATER**

**SAVE WATER THIS SUMMER**

We can't rely on rains to come.
Every drop counts.

Western Cape
Government

BETTER TOGETHER

For water saving tips visit
www.h20hero.co.za

This sign, put up by the government, encourages citizens to save water in Prince Albert, South Africa.

People carried water collected from a natural spring in Cape Town, South Africa, in January 2018, as the city suffered one of the worst droughts in its recent history.

A boy drinks recycled wastewater at a recycling facility in California, U.S.A.

# WATER SAVING IDEAS THAT MADE A SPLASH

## CHECK OUT SOME OF THE WAYS PEOPLE HAVE TRIED TO SAVE WATER.

 ### RECYCLING OF WASTEWATER

Wastewater is any water that has already been used. This includes water that has been used in a factory, pumping through machine parts and pipes; water that goes down your sink drain; and yes—water that has been flushed down the toilet. But because water scarcity is a growing concern, scientists have developed ways to clean and reuse wastewater so that it can be used again as drinking water!

### DESALINATION »

In places around the world where fresh-water is scarce, people have turned to salt water as a possible option. The problem? People can't drink salt water because it would make them very sick. So through a scientific process called desalination, the salt is removed from the water, leaving—voilà!—freshwater. A potential drawback to desalination, however, is that the process can be quite expensive and uses a lot of energy, which could contribute to climate change. But some scientists and innovators are trying to figure out ways to

make it more accessible, cost-effective, and energy efficient. One big idea they're exploring is how to harness solar energy to power some desalination units.

### « SHADE BALLS

In 2015, 96 million "shade balls" were dumped into a reservoir in Los Angeles, a source for freshwater for the California city. The community was suffering from a serious drought, and the idea was that these four-inch (10-cm) black plastic balls, which floated on the top of the reservoir, would prevent water loss due to evaporation and keep out harmful reactions that could be triggered by too much sunlight. Eventually, the balls, which were a controversial choice that made news around the world, were replaced with more standard floating covers.

# WOMEN, GIRLS, and WATER

**IN MANY COUNTRIES AROUND THE WORLD WHERE CLEAN FRESHWATER IS NOT AVAILABLE INSIDE THE HOME, WOMEN AND GIRLS ARE OFTEN THE ONES TASKED WITH COLLECTING WATER.** In fact, in eight out of 10 households, it is the women and girls' responsibility to collect water if it's not available in their home.

Worldwide, women and girls spend an estimated 200 million hours every day collecting water and 266 million hours finding a place to go to the bathroom.

Having access to clean water and sanitation is not just a health issue; it's an issue that keeps girls and boys from having equal opportunities.

For example, to collect water for the family, women and girls sometimes have to wake up in the middle of the night to begin their walk to the water source. And this walk can take hours.

When young girls are spending this much time each day collecting water, it often makes it more difficult, or even impossible, for them to go to school and get an education.

In many countries, girls begin participating in the daily trek to collect water as soon as they're able to walk.

REDUCING THE TIME IT TAKES TO GET WATER FROM **30 TO 15 MINUTES INCREASED GIRLS'** SCHOOL ATTENDANCE BY **12 PERCENT,** ACCORDING TO A STUDY IN TANZANIA.

Women and girls around the world, like this child on the outskirts of Sana'a, Yemen, are responsible for collecting water.

# WAR AND WATER

**IN 2011, A WAR BEGAN IN THE COUNTRY OF SYRIA, WHICH IS IN SOUTHWESTERN ASIA.** Since then, more than 13.4 million people there have fled their homes trying to stay safe. Some of them went to neighboring countries, while others went to different locations within Syria to escape the violence that was happening where they lived.

In Teir Maleh, a small village in Syria, some residents returned after having been away for more than two years. When they arrived back to their homes, the ways they used to get water—from pipes and water tanks—had all been destroyed by the war. This meant that people in the village had no access to freshwater. And they weren't alone. In that region, called north rural Homs, 50,000 people were left without access to drinking water for four years.

To get water, the people living in the village had to buy expensive water that private companies delivered in trucks. This was very hard, because many of the community members had very little money, and they needed to use the money they had to repair their homes and businesses that had been destroyed by the war.

The villagers often had to make really difficult choices, like giving up cleaning and bathing so that they had water to drink. And sometimes, they even had to drink water out of wells that they knew were dirty because they had no other options.

"Water was in short supply and of poor quality," says Bayan, a 14-year-old girl who lives in Teir Maleh. "It gave me kidney problems. It also meant we had to ration water to the extreme. My mother wouldn't let my younger siblings play outside so that we didn't use too much water showering and doing laundry."

However, UNICEF, an organization that works to protect the rights of children around the world and help improve their lives, recently installed a water pumping system in their village. Each day, families walk to the waterspout and fill up large cans of water to use and drink.

While the people living in Teir Maleh are grateful and happy to now have safe access to clean freshwater, it's important to remember what is at stake for people living in areas where there is war. Very often they experience limited access to resources that many people around the world take for granted, things such as food, water, and energy.

Relief groups such as the International Committee of the Red Cross (ICRC) deliver aid to those affected by war.

**WAR** DENIES PEOPLE ACCESS TO **ESSENTIAL RESOURCES,** INCLUDING **WATER.**

# BRINGING WATER TO THOSE IN NEED

## Q & A With Georgie Badiel

>> **G**eorgie Badiel grew up between Burkina Faso and the village of Koffikro in Ivory Coast, West Africa, and began making the daily trek for water even before she could walk. Strapped to her grandmother's back, she would travel miles to reach the nearest water source. Then, as soon as she was big enough, she began walking during the several-hour journey, carrying small containers of water back to her village.

Many people in Burkina Faso—some estimates say nearly 10 million people—live without clean water, and culturally it is considered the job of women to collect water for their family. This means that women and young girls wake before the sun rises to travel miles to their nearest water source, which is often contaminated with bacteria.

In 2003, Georgie was crowned Miss Burkina Faso in a national beauty pageant, and then the following year, Miss Africa. After that, she traveled to Paris, France, to begin an international modeling career. Eventually, she moved to New York City, where she lives now.

In 2015, Georgie started the Georgie Badiel Foundation, a charitable organization that works to bring clean water to Burkina Faso by building, maintaining, and restoring wells. Georgie also co-created the inspiring children's book *The Water Princess*, which is based on her life, and wrote its sequel, *Water Is Here*.

Georgie Badiel is on a mission to bring clean water to more people in Burkina Faso.

### Q: When you were little, what did you think of going to collect water?

When you [first] start walking, [you are given] a small bucket and then the bucket gets bigger and bigger and bigger. At eight years old, I became kind of like a rebel. Because one thing I did not like was that me and my girl cousins would go fetch the water while the boys were sleeping. To me, it was unacceptable.

In my culture and in many African cultures, [anything] concerning taking care of the home is the woman's responsibility. Growing up with five brothers, [I thought], *If we all have to use it, if we all need it, why don't we all go? Why do I have to go get water for them?* I didn't like it at all.

### Q: How would you use the water that you collected?

First, we would boil the water and filter it. Then, we would use it to cook, wash our clothes, clean the house, shower, and drink. We were very careful [about] the ways that we would use the water because every drop counts.

### Q: What inspired you to start the Georgie Badiel Foundation?

After living and working in all these beautiful places—Paris, New York, London, and Milan—and after having this fabulous life, I went back home to Burkina Faso to visit my sister, who was almost nine months pregnant. And every day, she had to wake up between 2 a.m. and 4 a.m. to begin walking to get water. To me that was like a reality check. I couldn't believe that people still had to do that, that a woman who is almost about to give birth has to do that. It really touched my soul and that is when I decided to make a difference on the water issue.

### Q: The Georgie Badiel Foundation has helped to build 22 wells, including one solar-powered well, and restore 144 existing wells, and it has taught more than 175 women in the community how to fix broken wells and maintain them. Why was it important to you that the women be the ones to learn this skill?

Yes, we have reached 123 communities, including my father's village and my grandmother's village—providing water for more than 300,000 people! When I started the foundation in the beginning, I would get to villages and see that there was a broken well and women still had to walk three or four hours away to go get water. I would ask, "Why is this well not restored?" And they would tell me that they would have to pay someone to restore the well and it was too expensive, that they didn't have enough money. So I thought, *All right, if water is still considered a woman's problem, let's empower women to solve the problem.*

And you're going to laugh because everywhere we go now to teach women to restore and maintain the well, men want to be a part of it! They say, "Why would you exclude us? We want to be part of it, too"—so that's very exciting.

### Q: How have you seen people's lives change through the work you are doing?

When it comes to education, I love to see how children [are doing] better at school. Now that young girls no longer have to fetch water before they go to school, attendance is up and they have better results.

I have villages where women actually use the water to start a small garden, so they provide food for their family, they sell their vegetables [at] the market, and they're more independent. [They're empowered to do more than] fetch the water and count on their husbands to take care of the family, and the men respect them more. When it comes to health, in communities where there is a well, there are less reports of [waterborne] diseases such as diarrhea.

What I am personally doing with the Georgie Badiel Foundation is bigger than me. We really want to change Burkina Faso by bringing the basic necessities. And, hopefully, once we achieve that goal, we will take that same goal to other countries that need water. Water has an impact on every part of life. Water is life.

# FRESHWATER and FARMING

 **THE GREATEST USE OF FRESHWATER AROUND THE WORLD IS NOT FOR DRINKING OR BATHING BUT FOR FARMING.** In fact, about 70 percent of the freshwater used on Earth goes toward growing the fruits and vegetables we eat, producing plants like hay and grass, and raising farm animals.

**Did You Know ...**

- In places where it rains less, farmers must withdraw more water from local freshwater sources to water their crops.

- Giving crops water to help them grow is called irrigation. Irrigation is thought to have started more than 7,500 years ago in Mesopotamia (an area in southwest Asia, where the first human civilization is thought to have started).

- The three countries that use the most water for irrigation are China, India, and the United States.

- Worldwide, the leading water-consuming grains are wheat and rice.

One way that farmers can use less water is by planting crops that grow well in the climate where they're located. For example, if farmers live somewhere that gets little rainfall throughout the year, it's a good idea to plant crops that require less water to thrive so they rely less on freshwater.

## DRY FARMING

In areas that receive little rain, one technique that some water-conscious farmers use is called "dry farming." This is a method that uses no irrigation—only natural rainfall. Farmers choose and plant crops that require little water, and then they rely solely on rain and the moisture that remains in the soil from the wet season to supply water to their crops during the dry season. The world's soil holds about eight times as much water as all of its rivers combined. The trick is figuring out how to make the best use of this moisture without wasting any.

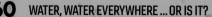

A field irrigation sprinkler system waters lettuce crops in central California, U.S.A.

## A GOLD STAR CHART FOR GROWN-UPS!

In the United States, the government has established a set of "Best Management Practices," or BMPs, regarding water use for businesses and farmers. Each positive practice that businesses and farms apply—such as limiting phosphorus runoff, using fertilizer properly, capturing and recycling rainwater—earns them a certain number of points.

# MAKE RAIN CLOUDS

## Done right, this experiment provides the most rewarding *whoosh*.

### ⚠ GRAB A GROWN-UP!

Ask a parent or adult supervisor for help and use extra caution when working with tools such as knives, scissors, or other sharp objects.

This experiment mimics the part of Earth's water cycle in which evaporated water (water vapor) cools and condenses, forming clouds as it connects with dust. In this experiment, the alcohol acts like the dust, providing something cool for water droplets to attach to.

When you pressurize the soda bottle by pumping air in, the air molecules collide with each other and warm the bottle. Releasing the pressure causes the water vapor to condense quickly, forming a cloud.

### YOU WILL NEED
- Safety goggles
- Cork (such as one from a wine bottle)
- 2-liter soda bottle with cap, clean and dry
- Bicycle pump with needle
- Large sewing needle, skewer, drill bit, or any tool or object that can make a hole big enough for the pump needle to go through the cork
- 1 teaspoon (5 mL) of rubbing alcohol
- Optional: duct tape

### GLITCH?
No cloud? That's probably because your seal isn't tight enough. Try a different cork or use duct tape to tighten the seal.

### BONUS: REVERSE THE EXPERIMENT!
Before the cloud disappears, put the pump needle back in and pump a couple more times. The cloud should disappear as quickly as it appeared. Release the pressure, and the cloud will form again.

**STEP 1:**
Put on your safety goggles. Fit your cork to your bottle. You may need to shave the sides off the cork to get a tight fit. Your aim here is to make the tightest possible seal. Then trim the cork to the length of the bike pump needle. You want the needle to be able to pass through the cork into the bottle while maintaining a tight seal.

**STEP 2:**
Make a path for the bicycle pump needle using your skewer, drill bit, or sewing needle. Be sure the object you use to pierce the cork is narrower than the bike pump needle, or you won't have a tight seal. When the cork is ready, take it out of the bottle.

**STEP 3:**
Pour the rubbing alcohol into the bottle and screw the cap back on.

**STEP 4:**
With the cap on, lay the bottle on its side, and roll it so that the alcohol sloshes around and coats the inside of the bottle thoroughly and evenly.

**STEP 5:**
Remove the cap and insert the cork.

**STEP 6:**
Insert the bike pump needle in the cork. Pump four or five times. The cork might pop out immediately, creating the reaction, and a cloud will form in the bottle. But you might have to pump a few more times, then stop and pull the needle out. The inside of the bottle should start to look cloudy. And there you have it: Your very own rain cloud in a bottle!

**SAFETY NOTE:**
AIM THE BOTTLE AWAY FROM YOU AND ANYONE ELSE.

**WHAT TO EXPECT:**
ONCE THE PRESSURE IS RELEASED—EITHER BECAUSE THE CORK POPS OUT OR THE NEEDLE IS REMOVED—A CLOUD SHOULD FORM QUICKLY AND DRAMATICALLY IN THE BOTTLE.

③

⑤

⑥

# H₂-Oh-Wow!

## Check out this *WEIRD BUT TRUE* Water Wonder.

**Caño Cristales, COLOMBIA**

From May to November, when the water reaches a certain height, this typically crystal clear body of water will appear vibrant shades of yellow, green, blue, black, and red. The river has been called "the River of Five Colors," and "the Melted Rainbow." The source of this river's dazzling display is *Macarenia clavigera*, a delicate, lacelike aquatic plant that changes colors.

## CHAPTER 4

# Water Pollution ...

# AND SOME

# SOLUTIONS!

>> **THERE ARE AROUND EIGHT BILLION PEOPLE LIVING ON EARTH. WE ALL NEED WATER TO SURVIVE, WHICH MAKES WATER ONE OF THE WORLD'S MOST PRECIOUS RESOURCES.**

But only about 2.5 percent of the planet's freshwater is available for us to use. And of the freshwater that is available, much of it is not safe for drinking or other uses because of various types of pollution and contamination.

Pollution not only affects people; it has been devastating for fish and other aquatic organisms all over the globe. It's important to understand what negatively impacts water quality, especially because so many of the contaminants come from human activity. Read on to find out how—instead of contributing to the pollution—you can be part of the solution!

# A CLOSER LOOK AT WATER POLLUTION

**P**ollution is any substance present in an environment that causes harm or can make living things sick. Water pollution is usually caused by chemicals or microorganisms that contaminate a body of water.

## DIFFERENT SOURCES OF WATER POLLUTION

- **Groundwater** This is the water that exists belowground in aquifers. Almost 40 percent of Americans get their drinking water from groundwater. Groundwater can become polluted when chemicals, such as pesticides or fertilizers, soak into the soil and seep into aquifers.

- **Surface Water** About 60 percent of the freshwater that Americans use in their homes comes from surface water sources such as rivers and lakes. But it is estimated that nearly half of the rivers and streams in America and about one-third of the lakes are polluted and unfit for drinking, swimming, or fishing.

- **Ocean Water** About 80 percent of the pollution in the world's oceans comes from land and is then carried by streams and rivers out to the sea. Plastic and other litter is also blown by the wind into the ocean or travels there through storm drains and other waterways.

### AGRICULTURAL

In the United States, agriculture is the top source of contamination in rivers and streams, the second leading cause of pollution in wetlands, and the third leading cause of pollution in lakes. When it rains, fertilizer, pesticides, and animal waste from farms or from factories that house animals can wash into nearby waterways, bringing bacteria, viruses, and high levels of nutrients, like phosphorus and nitrogen with them. Nutrient pollution is the biggest threat to water quality worldwide. (For more on nutrient pollution, see pp. 80–81.)

# DIFFERENT TYPES OF WATER POLLUTION

## STORMWATER

This is the water that flows over surfaces, such as roads and parking lots, after it rains, carrying with it all of the litter and chemicals found on the ground, such as oil, dust, pizza crusts, and animal waste. Instead of soaking into the ground, this water flows back into surface water sources, such as lakes, rivers, and oceans.

## SEWAGE AND WASTEWATER

Wastewater is any water that has been used, such as the water from our sinks, showers, and toilets. In the United States, there are wastewater treatment facilities that clean and disinfect previously used water before it is discharged back into a river, lake, or ocean. But even still, sometimes high levels of stormwater cause sewers to overflow. Because of that, an estimated 850 billion gallons (3.2 trillion L) of untreated wastewater is released back into the environment every year. Worldwide, about 80 percent of wastewater flows directly back into the environment without any treatment.

## PLASTIC

If a piece of plastic is thrown on the ground or is carried by the wind from an overflowing trash can, it often makes its way to small bodies of water that empty into large bodies of water. Every year, more than eight million tons (7.3 million t) of plastic are dumped into the ocean. That's equal to two million large hippopotamuses!

## OIL

Sometimes huge ships carrying oil can cause large-scale, dangerous oil spills in the ocean. But nearly half of the oil that makes it into waterways comes from factories, farms, cities, and oil that drips from people's cars and trucks.

Peltier addresses the Global Landscapes Forum at the United Nations in 2019.

Autumn and her Great-Aunt Josephine

**A**utumn Peltier was eight years old when she learned that not everyone had access to clean, safe drinking water. It happened at an event at a First Nation community near her home in Ontario, Canada. In the bathroom were signs that said things like "Don't drink the water" and "Water not for consumption." When she asked about the signs later, her mom explained that many First Nation communities in Ontario must boil their water before drinking it, to kill harmful germs.

This really troubled Autumn, who is a member of the Wiikwemkoong First Nation and had grown up listening to her Great-Aunt Josephine, a water activist, talk about how sacred and precious water is. When Autumn was just 15, she was named chief water commissioner by the Anishinabek Nation, an advocacy group for 40 First Nations across Ontario, Canada. She has followed in her aunt's footsteps and has spoken all around the world—including at the United Nations, twice!—and is a renowned water activist. Here we talk about what motivates her courageous work.

**Q: How did your work as a water advocate and activist begin?**
There was a public speaking contest at my elementary school, and the topic was, "What means the most to you?" We had to write and deliver the speech in our language, which is Anishinaabemowin. My speech was about water and the environment. A few years later, I was invited to the Children's Climate Conference in Sweden, and then after that, the Assembly of First Nations Chief, in Deschênes, Quebec, wanted to hear what I had to say. From there, I was getting invitations from everywhere to speak and talk to kids about the environment.

**Q: Have you always been comfortable speaking in front of crowds?**
I was really scared to speak in front of people at first, but then I would think about my Great-Aunt Josephine. She used her voice because the water doesn't have a voice; it can't speak up. And if there are people that can't speak up or are too afraid, she did it for them, too. All I have to think about is that I'm speaking up for the water and my people. It gives me a lot of motivation.

**Q: Your great-aunt, Josephine Mandamin, was a water activist, and she walked the perimeter of all five Great Lakes to raise awareness for water issues. How has her work influenced you?**
I spent a lot of time with her since I was a baby and even attended some of her water walks with her. For as long as I can remember, she was teaching me that water is a precious resource.

**Q: What does it mean to you to be a water advocate?**
In my culture, water is one of our most sacred elements because water gives us life. We depend on water. We need it. For me, it's a really big role and I'm really happy to be able to carry on my Aunt Josephine's work, represent indigenous youth, and represent my people.

**Q: How do you educate yourself about this complicated issue?**
I do a lot of research and Googling, and I actually go and physically visit the places where there are boil-water advisories. There, I talk to the people and say, "I want to hear your perspective on the issue."

**Q: What would you like young people to know about how they can help?**
That anyone can do this work. It's always a stronger message when it's coming from more than one person, so I encourage other youth to speak up and advocate as well. There's a lot you can do.

**Q: When you talk to leaders and politicians, what do you want them to do to ensure First Nations communities have access to clean drinking water?**
I've been to so many meetings where a leader makes promises like, Yes we'll do this, yes we'll do that, but I want them to act now. I would like them to pay more attention to this issue and to realize how serious it is.

**Q: What do you want to do next?**
My goal is just to keep on doing this until I don't have to. That's exactly what my Aunt Josephine did. Nothing stopped her. About two days before she passed away, I visited her in the hospital and she told me, "Never stop doing the work, and never let anything stop you." I basically live by those words now.

Peltier at the 50th World Economic Forum annual meeting in Davos, Switzerland, in 2020

# FLINT, MICHIGAN

IN 2014, IN AN EFFORT TO SAVE MONEY, THE CITY OF FLINT, MICHIGAN, U.S.A., SWITCHED ITS FRESHWATER SOURCE. Instead of treated water from the Detroit Water and Sewerage Department (which came from Lake Huron and the Detroit River), the city began providing its citizens water from the Flint River. Right away, people noticed that the water that was coming out of the faucets in their homes smelled, tasted, and looked different. Some people even began getting skin rashes after they bathed. The city government, however, continued to tell its residents that the water was safe to drink, even after many tests showed dangerously high levels of lead in the water. Lead is a metal that when consumed can cause very serious health effects, especially for kids.

After these high levels of lead were discovered in the water, and blood tests showed high levels of lead in Flint residents' bodies, city officials finally admitted that they hadn't properly treated the water. As a result, the water was absorbing chemicals, metals, and bacteria from the pipes it was flowing through. A state of emergency was declared in the city, and residents began using water filters and bottled water for all their freshwater needs—including showering, brushing their teeth, cooking, and drinking.

In the years since the crisis began, the city switched back to the original water source, a new mayor vowed to replace all the lead water pipes with safer copper ones, and city officials said that tests show that the water is now safe to drink. But, understandably, Flint residents are still suspicious and scared. Many still drink only bottled water.

## RACE AND WATER INEQUALITY IN AMERICA

The population of Flint, Michigan, is more than 50 percent African American, and many residents felt that was why the government was not acting quickly enough or taking the situation seriously enough. It was suggested that if the citizens of Flint had been wealthy and white, this serious health concern would have been a top priority and they wouldn't have been exposed to these dangerous conditions for so long. This is called environmental racism, and statistics show that people of color and poor citizens are more likely to be exposed to environmental hazards than white and wealthy citizens.

According to a 2019 report on Americans' access to water, more than two million Americans don't have running water or indoor plumbing. And race was the strongest indicator of whether or not someone had running water. African American and Latinx households were nearly twice as likely as white Americans not to have running water or basic plumbing. And Native American households were 19 times more likely than the households of white Americans not to have running water or indoor plumbing.

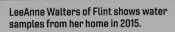

LeeAnne Walters of Flint shows water samples from her home in 2015.

# STANDING UP FOR SAFE DRINKING WATER

## Spotlight on Mari Copeny

In March of 2016, then eight-year-old Mari Copeny, a Flint, Michigan, resident, wrote a letter to President Barack Obama, who two months earlier had declared a state of emergency in Flint, asking him to meet with her. She wanted to share with him how the water crisis was affecting her and other kids like her. To her surprise, not only did President Obama write her back, he also visited her in Flint to see firsthand what was going on.

Justice is fairness—when all people are treated equally. Injustice is when a person, or a group of people, is treated unfairly or unequally. The activism of Mari Copeny shows us what is possible when a young person sees injustice and uses their unique voice to bring attention to it.

In the years since the water crisis began, Mari, also known as "Little Miss Flint," has continued to speak out and speak up for the people in her community. She is an inspiring activist, philanthropist, and public speaker, and she says in a decade or two, she'll be adding another title to her resume: president!

"I am one of the children that is affected by this water," Mari wrote to President Obama, "and I've been doing my best to march in protest and to speak out for all the kids who live here in Flint."

# WHERE DOES THE WATER GO WHEN ...

>> **You're standing at the sink,** washing all of the food grease and bits off the dishes after dinner ... ?

## OR

You flush the toilet after going to the bathroom ... ?

## OR

You're in the tub, soaking in a bubble bath. You lather up your hair and then rinse out the suds. Ready to get out, you release the plug, and the water swirls down the drain ... ?

## OR

Water is coursing through the pipes of a big machine, cooling hot parts in a giant factory, and when it's done it shoots off through a pipe in the wall ... ?

These are all examples of wastewater, water that is no longer clean because it has already been used and now contains a contaminant. What happens to this water next depends on where in the world you live. Sometimes that water flows through a series of pipes and directly into a natural body of water such as a river, lake, or ocean. Wastewater often contains harmful bacteria, chemicals, and nutrients that can potentially cause harm to animals and humans.

But in other places, this water is sent to a wastewater treatment facility, where it is purified before being sent back into a natural body of water or reused.

### SCREENS/DIGESTER

Water entering a wastewater treatment facility can contain all sorts of things, including branches, pieces of food, and litter! The first step is to screen out anything large that might have made its way in with the water. All the solid material removed from the wastewater is heated in enclosed tanks called "digesters." In the digesters, bacteria break down the materials. This reduces the amount of material, gets rid of disease-causing organisms, and eliminates some of the smelliness. After about 20 to 30 days, whatever is left is sent to landfills or used as fertilizer.

**CHLORINE**
Finally, the wastewater flows into a large tank where chlorine is added to the water to kill bacteria. Other chemicals are then added to neutralize the remaining chlorine, since it could harm fish and marine organisms if left in the water.

**GRIT**
Grit (things like coffee grounds and dirt), sludge (such as mud), and scum (things like grease, oil, and soap) are all removed from the water.

**AERATION**
Next, the remaining water is shaken up and exposed to air. This causes some of the dissolved gases (the ones that smell like rotten eggs and taste bad) to be released from the water. This aeration process also adds oxygen back into the water.

# THE STRAIGHT TRUTH ABOUT STRAIGHT PIPES

## Spotlight on Stella Bowles

**W**hen Stella Bowles was 11 years old, she heard a term she'd never heard before: "straight pipes." It was at the dinner table, and her mom was talking about how there were some that emptied into the LaHave River, right behind her family's house in Nova Scotia, Canada.

When Stella asked what that phrase meant, her mother explained that straight pipes are pipes that carry all the water and waste from people's toilets directly into the river, without any sort of filtration.

Stella was shocked.

"I started asking so many questions," Stella says, "like: How many are there? Is it safe to swim in the water? Why is this happening? Is this legal?"

Stella learned that straight pipes are not legal in Canada, but the government hadn't been strictly enforcing the law. She decided to make this topic the subject of her Grade 6 Science Fair project, but first she needed more information! So her mother reached out to a local organization, Coastal Action, who introduced them to Dr. David Maxwell, a local retired medical doctor who was also concerned by this issue. Dr. Maxwell became Stella's mentor, and together they set out to find answers to some of Stella's questions.

### STELLA THE SCIENTIST

"I've always really, really enjoyed science. My dad is very science-y. Together, we've made rockets in the backyard, little bubble machines, magic mud ... we even did one experiment where we turned on a light-bulb with electrodes and a pickle!"

**THIS RIVER IS CONTAMINATED WITH FECAL BACTERIA**

Stella and Dr. Maxwell

**Step 1: They put the water to the test.** To test for fecal bacteria in the water, Stella says, "We took samples from the river in four locations and we used a sterilized jar so that there were no other cross contaminants. Then, we brought each sample back home and ran it through a filter funnel. You pour the water in the top part, and then you suck the water through the filter in the middle. The water ends up on the bottom and all the bacteria is left on the top of the filter. Next, the filter goes on an enterococci testing card [to test for the presence of fecal bacteria], which then goes in an incubator for 36 hours. It's pretty cool because we grow fecal bacteria in our basement! My mom doesn't think that's cool, but I kinda think it's cool."

**Step 2: They received the results.** If there is fecal bacteria present in the sample, blue dots will appear on the testing card. "Each dot is a colony of fecal bacteria," Stella says. "If there are 70 dots, you shouldn't swim in the water. And anything over 170 dots, you should not even get the water in contact with your skin. In our town of Bridgewater, there were so many dots that the cards were uncountable. There were more than 1,000 dots."

**Step 3: They got the word out—big-time!** "When I got the results, I wanted my mom to pull over the car so I could tell people to get out of the water," Stella says. "When she said she wouldn't, I asked if I could have a Facebook page to post the results. She said, 'No, you're 11, you can't have a Facebook page.' So we compromised and put up a huge sign in front of our wharf, and it said, 'This River Is Contaminated With Fecal Bacteria.' As soon as we put that out, we had neighbors and members of the media at our door asking what it meant."

Within a few months, multiple government officials reached out to Stella to discuss this important issue, one that had captured the attention of her close-knit community. "I think they got together and said, 'OK, how are we going to take on this kid?'" Stella says. "The community was really angry with the results—not at me, but at the adults who weren't doing anything."

Before Stella began spreading the word about the results of her research, there were 600 straight pipes that emptied into the LaHave River. Since Stella's activism, the government has helped replace 140 straight pipes with septic systems, and they've set a goal of replacing 100 more each year, for six years. By 2023 they want to have all of the original 600 replaced with septic systems.

"One day, as my dad and I were walking into a store, this random gentleman was like, 'Yeah, Stella! Clean up that river,'" Stella says. "And I was like, 'Wow, thank you!' It has been amazing to see the whole community come together to tackle this huge issue. It wasn't just me. I got the ball rolling, but after that the community kept the ball rolling. It's kind of beautiful."

## STELLA'S TIPS FOR OTHER KIDS WHO WANT TO MAKE A DIFFERENCE

- Know that your age doesn't define what you can and cannot do.
- Work with a mentor.
- Remember, social media can be used for so much good, as long as you keep it positive.
- If you're passionate about something and you put your mind to it, then you can make it happen.

# ALL ABOUT ALGAL BLOOMS

>> **NUTRIENTS ARE SUBSTANCES THAT NOURISH LIVING THINGS AND HELP THEM TO GROW AND STAY HEALTHY.** For example, vitamins, water, and protein are all nutrients that humans need. So it would be understandable to think that more nutrients mean healthier living things. But that's not always the case. In fact, in high quantities, certain nutrients can become (very!) unhealthy.

Nitrogen and phosphorus are two nutrients that in high doses cause serious environmental problems. Nitrogen and phosphorus are found in fertilizers, animal manure, human waste, and some cleaning detergents. When it rains, these nutrients can mix with water and flow out to surface water sources such as lakes, rivers, streams, and oceans.

Then, when the nitrogen and phosphorus encounter warm water, calm winds, and sunlight, algae (a type of nonflowering plant) in the water quickly multiply, creating a large area of algae cover called a "bloom." Harmful Algal Blooms (HABs) produce toxins that can be dangerous—and lethal—to fish and animals, and that can make humans sick.

People are advised not to swim in water where there is an HAB, and often bodies of water and beaches that are experiencing one will close to the public. HABs can happen with different species of algae, leading to different color blooms. One common HAB is called "red tide," due to the red color of the water during blooms of a certain species of algae called *Karenia brevis.* Red tide blooms in Florida have become a persistent problem for both wildlife and humans.

Red tide in Acapulco, Mexico

TO REDUCE **HARMFUL ALGAL BLOOMS,** PEOPLE SHOULD USE **FERTILIZERS** ONLY WHEN THEY'RE SURE THEIR LAWNS DON'T HAVE ENOUGH NUTRIENTS.

## WHAT ARE "DEAD ZONES"?

Dead zones are areas in bodies of water where Harmful Algal Blooms have caused the levels of oxygen in the water to become so low that living things can't survive. While dead zones can happen all over the world, they usually happen in locations with a high volume of runoff from farms and factories (and therefore high levels of nitrogen and phosphorus). There is a huge dead zone in the Gulf of Mexico that varies in size from year to year, sometimes extending 8,500 square miles (22,000 sq km)—about the size of the U.S. state of New Jersey. The dead zone is located where the Mississippi River flows into the Gulf of Mexico. The Mississippi River contains lots of runoff from farms and stormwater from cities.

There are estimated to be hundreds of dead zones around the world, and the bad news is they seem to be growing in size. The good news is they can be reversed. But to do it, we will need to prioritize decreasing the amounts of nitrogen and phosphorus pollution in Earth's bodies of water.

# MAKE A WATER FILTER

## This fun science experiment turns dirty water clean ... well, kind of.

### ⚠ GRAB A GROWN-UP!
Ask a parent or adult supervisor for help, and use extra caution when working with tools such as knives, scissors, or other sharp objects.

How do you clean up dirty water?

Not with soap! You need a filter, which is a device that removes impurities from water. The filter you'll make here is a super strainer, and it'll help you clean up your act. Make sure you have the help of an adult before you begin.

### YOU WILL NEED
- 2-liter plastic bottle, empty and clean
- Utility knife
- Coffee filter (A bandanna, old sock, napkin, or paper towel works, too!)
- As many of the following filter materials as you can get: activated charcoal (available in the fish section at a pet store), gravel, sand (coarse and/or fine), cotton balls
- Dirty water (make your own with stuff like coffee grounds, dirt, crunched-up old leaves, cooking oil, or tiny pieces of foam)
- Spoon
- Measuring cup
- Stopwatch or clock with a second hand
- Pencil and paper

**STEP 1:**
Ask a grown-up to cut the bottle in half. Then flip the bottle's top half over and put it in the bottom, so the top looks like a funnel. You'll build your filter in the top part.

**STEP 2:**
Place the coffee filter (or a sock, bandanna, etc.) at the bottom of your filter.

**STEP 3:**
Add cotton balls, charcoal, gravel, sand, and/or other materials in layers. You can use just one of them or all of them. Tip: Think about which order to add them. Bigger filter materials usually catch bigger impurities.

**STEP 4:**
Write down which filter materials you used and in what order you layered them.

**STEP 5:**
Stir your dirty water and measure out a cup of it.

### WHAT'S GOING ON?

**THE SLOWER, THE BETTER!** The longer it takes for water to move through a filter, the cleaner the water gets. Water itself slips easily through the filter materials, but bigger gunk, like dirt, gets trapped. The filter materials usually get finer and finer, so they can catch whatever the previous layer missed. Activated charcoal can be near the end of the water's path, because it uses an electrical charge to grab particles too small for us to see.

### STEP 6:
Get your timer ready!

### STEP 7:
Pour a cup of dirty water into your filter. Start the timer as soon as you begin pouring.

### STEP 8:
Time how long it takes for all the water to go through the filter. Then write down how long it took.

**WARNING!**
YOUR FILTERED WATER IS NOT CLEAN ENOUGH TO DRINK.

### STEP 9:
Carefully scoop out the filter materials, one layer at a time. What did each layer take out of the water?

### STEP 10:
Keep experimenting! Clean the bottle and try again. Put the filter materials in a different order each time. What do you discover?

# H₂-Oh-Wow!

## Check out this WEIRD BUT TRUE Water Wonder.

### Lake Natron, TANZANIA

This lake contains a rare mix of naturally occurring ingredients that make for a very inhospitable environment. It has both salt and alkali (a corrosive chemical compound) because of the high amounts of the chemical natron that enter the lake via runoff from a nearby volcano. Very few things are able to live here due to the super harsh conditions—including temperatures that can reach 140°F (60°C)! When animals happen to die in the lake—for example, when birds fly into its highly reflective surface—they calcify, perfectly (and eerily!) preserving their carcasses and turning them into spooky and stunning statues.

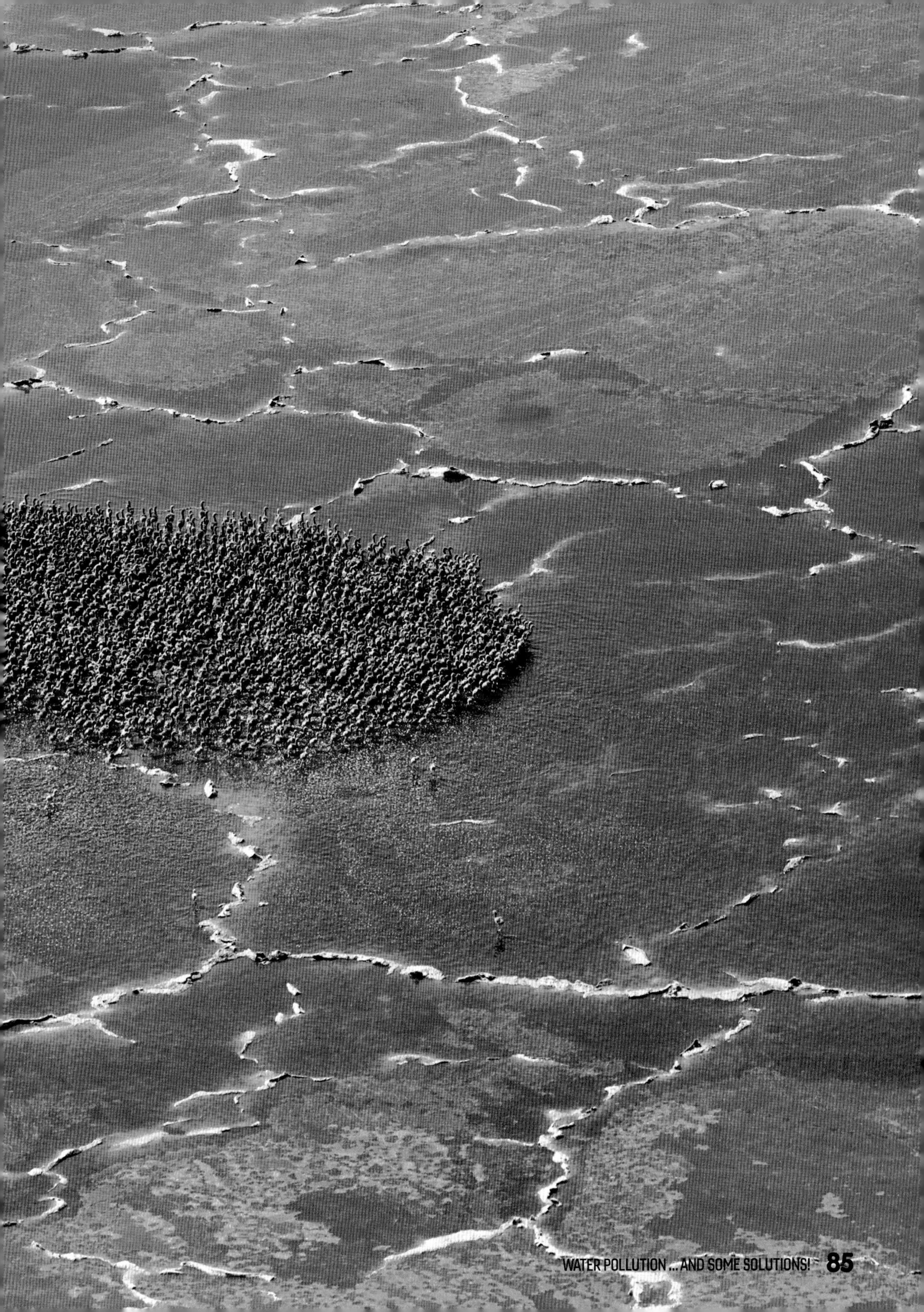

**CHAPTER 5**

# A CHANGING CLIMATE

» **YOU'VE PROBABLY HEARD PEOPLE TALKING ABOUT CLIMATE CHANGE AND WONDERED WHAT IT IS, EXACTLY, AND WHAT—IF ANYTHING—IT HAS TO DO WITH YOU.** Climate change is the warming or cooling of Earth and the changing of its climate. While some climate change is naturally occurring, what we are experiencing now is the result of human activities.

But there's so much we can all do to *help* the planet—read on to learn more!

Extreme weather events, like the hurricane pictured here, are going to become increasingly common as Earth's average temperature rises.

# What Is CLIMATE CHANGE?

>> **HUMAN ACTIVITY IS CAUSING THE CLIMATE CHANGE WE ARE EXPERIENCING NOW: THE WARMING OF EARTH AND THE CHANGING OF WEATHER AND CLIMATE PATTERNS.**

One of the biggest contributors to climate change is the burning of fossil fuels. Fossil fuels include coal, oil, and natural gas. Humans all around the world burn these fuels to power electricity generation, to heat homes and businesses, and to fuel different means of transportation, such as cars, planes, trains, and cruise ships.

When fossil fuels are burned, they emit gases known as greenhouse gases. These gases—such as carbon dioxide and chlorofluorocarbons—create a sort of blanket around our planet, trapping the heat inside the atmosphere and causing the planet to warm. In moderation, greenhouse gases are good. Without any, Earth would be a big ball of ice!

The burning of fossil fuels to generate power and to fuel transportation contributes to climate change.

HUMAN **ACTIVITY** IS CAUSING EARTH TO WARM AND ITS CLIMATE TO CHANGE. BUT THERE ARE THINGS WE CAN DO TO HELP!

# How Climate Change IMPACTS WATER

As EARTH WARMS, there are big-time RIPPLE EFFECTS on the water cycle and our planet's water systems. Here are a few of them.

**WARMER AIR HOLDS MORE WATER** As the atmosphere heats up, more water evaporates from oceans, lakes, rivers, soil, and plants. Because warmer air can hold more water than cooler air, when precipitation does fall, there can be more of it, causing heavier rainfall, snowfall, and floods.

**THE MELTING OF GLACIAL ICE** As temperatures have risen, glaciers have begun to melt faster than they can be replenished by snow. This melt is a contributor to rising sea levels. »

**IRREGULAR CHANGE IN SEASONS** In some areas, warm, spring-like weather is happening earlier in the year than usual, causing ice and snow to melt earlier. Then, come summer and fall, there is less freshwater available.

**OCEAN ACIDIFICATION** As humans burn fossil fuels, carbon dioxide ($CO_2$) is released into the air. About 30 percent of the $CO_2$ is absorbed by Earth's oceans, causing them to become more acidic. The impact of this change in the chemistry of the ocean is not totally known yet, but it has already been shown to negatively impact coral reefs and to cause the shells on certain organisms such as clams, mussels, and shrimp to dissolve. ≫

≪ **MORE FREQUENT AND SEVERE DROUGHTS** On some parts of the planet, warmer temperatures have caused more evaporation and drier land, spurring an increase in droughts and wildfires.

**A RISE IN OCEAN TEMPERATURES** Oceans absorb 93 percent of the heat trapped by greenhouse gases, so as climate change has increased, so too has the temperature of the ocean. Warmer waters can create an environment too harsh for some species, such as coral reefs, to survive—causing disruptions to entire ecosystems. Warmer ocean temperatures also contribute to stronger hurricanes. And because warmer water takes up more room than cooler water—what is known as "thermal expansion"—sea levels rise. ≫

≪ **DIFFERENT, UNEVEN WEATHER PATTERNS** A changing climate means that some places on the planet will get drier, while other places will experience wetter conditions. A warmer atmosphere may also cause more severe weather events, such as tornadoes and hurricanes.

# WATER WARRIOR
# A CHAMPION FOR CLIMATE CHANGE
## Spotlight on Greta Thunberg

Inspired by Greta Thunberg, students in Sydney, Australia, gathered in 2018 to demand their government take action on climate change.

## THE PARIS AGREEMENT

In 2015, leaders from nearly 200 countries around the world agreed to a historic pact called the Paris Agreement. The leaders agreed to decrease the amount of greenhouse gases emitted by their countries in an effort to stop Earth's temperature from continuing to rise.

**W**hat began as one girl sitting alone outside a government building grew into a worldwide movement to protect the planet.

In 2018, Greta Thunberg, who was 15 years old at the time, decided to begin a weeks-long strike to get the attention of leaders in the country where she lives, Sweden. Day after day, Greta sat on the cobblestones outside the parliament building with her hand-painted sign that read "SKOLSTREJK FÖR KLIMATET," which translates to "school strike for climate." What she wanted was simple: tougher government policies to ensure that fewer greenhouse gases would be emitted into the atmosphere.

Inspired by Greta, kids around the world soon began staying out of school on Fridays to protest, and the movement and hashtag #FridaysForFuture was born.

In 2019, several same-day climate rallies were held all around the world. During one in May, more than 2,300 school strikes took place in more than 130 countries. From Uganda and Italy to South Korea and New Zealand, young people joined together to show the world how important it is that every-one, everywhere, do everything they can to combat climate change and fight for the future health of our planet.

# WINNING WATER IDEA: SPONGE CITIES

## Check out these smart, water-saving strategies that China is putting to use.

In many cities around the world, as the number of people living and working in them increases, many wetlands, green spaces, and bodies of water are being replaced by new buildings, parking lots, and roads. As a result, when it rains, the water has fewer places to go. Without grass to soak into, or a lake to land in, the water gathers and causes flooding. In China, the number of cities that have experienced flooding has more than doubled since 2008.

China, however, has found a really cool way to help solve this problem—sponge cities!

Just like a sponge, these Chinese cities are being designed to absorb water, with the hope that they can capture and reuse up to 70 percent of the rain that falls there. To do this, the government has planted gardens on the rooftops of buildings, created new wetlands and small bodies of water where water can be stored, and installed sidewalks that soak up water, absorbing it into the earth.

**Permeable pavement** is porous, which means it has tiny little spaces that allow water to soak in below the surface, where it can slowly be absorbed by the soil below.

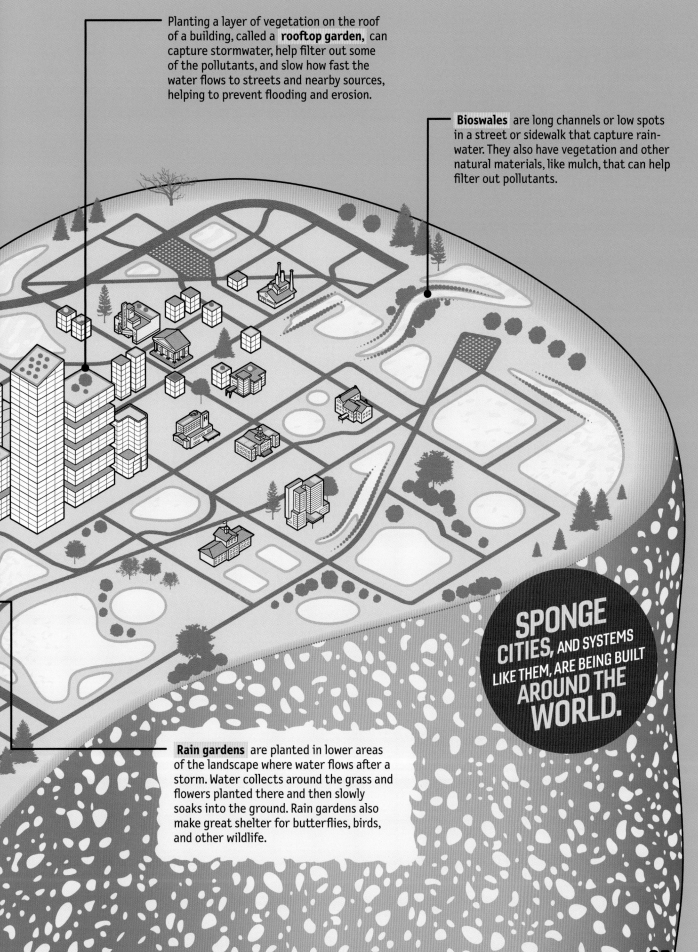

Planting a layer of vegetation on the roof of a building, called a **rooftop garden,** can capture stormwater, help filter out some of the pollutants, and slow how fast the water flows to streets and nearby sources, helping to prevent flooding and erosion.

**Bioswales** are long channels or low spots in a street or sidewalk that capture rainwater. They also have vegetation and other natural materials, like mulch, that can help filter out pollutants.

**Rain gardens** are planted in lower areas of the landscape where water flows after a storm. Water collects around the grass and flowers planted there and then slowly soaks into the ground. Rain gardens also make great shelter for butterflies, birds, and other wildlife.

SPONGE CITIES, AND SYSTEMS LIKE THEM, ARE BEING BUILT AROUND THE WORLD.

# 10 EVERYDAY THINGS YOU CAN DO TO COMBAT CLIMATE CHANGE

TO HELP COMBAT CLIMATE CHANGE, do what you can to reduce your CARBON FOOTPRINT. Your carbon footprint is the amount of GREENHOUSE GASES released into Earth's atmosphere as a result of your activities. Here are some simple ways to do that.

**1** Use less air-conditioning in the summer and less heat in the winter. Open windows to cool off and bundle up to keep warm! »

**2** Whenever you can, walk or bike, or take public transportation to your destination instead of riding in a car.

**3** Turn off lights when you leave a room. The electricity used in your house is created by burning fossil fuels, which releases high amounts of the greenhouse gas carbon dioxide into the environment.

**4** If you're going to be idling for more than 10 seconds—maybe you're waiting in a drive-thru or picking someone up from school—encourage the adult driving to turn off the car. »

**5** Encourage your family to swap old incandescent light-bulbs for LEDs or the new compact fluorescent lights (CFLs). They use only 25 percent as much electricity and provide the same amount of light. And they last 10 times longer. »

**6** Turn off electrical items, such as computers and TVs, when you're not using them.

**7** Recycle! Creating new items from scratch—whether clothes, appliances, or water bottles—requires a tremendous amount of energy, which emits greenhouse gases into the atmosphere.

**8** Reduce your food waste. It's estimated that nearly one-third of the food produced in the world goes to waste. And when we waste food, we also waste the massive amounts of energy and water that are used to grow it and then get it to your grocery store! »

**9** Replace single-use items (items that are meant to be used once and then thrown away), such as plastic straws and disposable water bottles, with reusable versions, such as stainless steel straws and water bottles.

**10** Write or visit your local officials and let them know how important climate change is to you!

# H₂-Oh-Wow!

## Check out this *WEIRD BUT TRUE* Water Wonder.

## The Boiling River, PERU

The seemingly miraculous Boiling River in the jungles of Peru reaches temperatures of more than 200°F (93.3°C). A human would be badly burned if they were to fall in, and when small mammals, reptiles, and amphibians do, they likely don't survive. The reason the river, which is a tributary of the Amazon, is so hot is because of geothermal energy, or energy stored deep inside Earth, which drives heat from the planet's core out to the surface.

# CHAPTER 6

# Saving the
# WORLD'S
# OCEANS

» **EARTH'S OCEANS ARE AMONG OUR PLANET'S GREATEST TREASURES.** They are filled with a universe of magnificent marine life, from the largest mammal in the world (the blue whale) to small supernatural-looking creatures, like the Christmas tree worm, the pink see-through fantasia, the leafy sea dragon, and the super slimy blobfish.

The oceans are also necessary to our survival: The plants that live in them produce a majority of the world's oxygen and absorb carbon dioxide from our atmosphere. And oceans help regulate weather patterns and our climate by moving heat from the Equator to the poles.

Oceans are amazing and important, and they are also seriously impacted by environmental problems like climate change and plastic pollution. Turn the page to learn more about the problem—and what you can do to help.

Though we can see their colorful crowns, most of the Christmas tree worms' bodies are deep inside holes they tunneled into the live coral.

# 10 AWESOME FACTS ABOUT OCEANS

**1** About 70 percent of the surface of Earth is covered by ocean.

**2** About 97 percent of the world's water is in the oceans.

**3** Scientists estimate that about one million species of animals live in the oceans.

**4** About 70 percent of the oxygen we breathe is produced by plants in the oceans.

**5** We have only explored about 5 percent of the world's oceans. There's a lot more to be discovered!

 **6** The moon's gravity causes the water on Earth that's nearest to it to bulge out, causing a high tide. Coastal areas experience two high and two low tides each day, depending on where they are in relation to the moon's gravitational pull.

**7** It is estimated that there are 321,003,271 cubic miles (1,338,000,000 cu km) of water in the oceans. That's equal to about 352,670,000,000,000,000,000,000 gallons of milk!

**8** The Pacific Ocean is the largest ocean in the world, covering about 65,100,000 square miles (168,600,000 sq km). On average, it's about 13,386 feet (4,080 m) deep.

**10** There are about 32,000 living fish species. That's more than the total of all other vertebrate species (amphibians, reptiles, birds, and mammals) combined!

 **9** The deepest part of the ocean is the Mariana Trench, in the Pacific Ocean. At its deepest, it extends almost seven miles (11 km) down.

# THE OCEAN'S PLASTIC PROBLEM

**PLASTIC IS A MATERIAL THAT WAS CREATED IN THE 1850s.** For years, this breakthrough invention was thought to make life safer, simpler, and easier. And while this was true for a time, we really overdid it. We made, used, and threw away a ton of plastic. Well, way more than a ton, actually. Since 1950, humans have created more than nine billion tons (8.2 billion t) of plastic. And today, plastic is one of the greatest environmental hazards of our time.

Unfortunately, Earth's oceans—and the many marine animals that live in them—are greatly impacted by all that plastic. Every year, an estimated 8.8 million tons (8 million t) of plastic ends up in the oceans. That's equal to about 275,000 large garbage trucks! Plastic travels via rivers, streams, and storm drains; it is carried by the wind; it's dropped by boaters and beachgoers; and it breaks up into tiny pieces, called microplastics, that find their way into the oceans.

Animals in the oceans often get tangled up in plastic pollution, and they accidentally eat it, mistaking it for food. Plastic has been found in the bellies of whales, dolphins, turtles, and fish—yep, like the ones we eat.

## FLOATING ISLANDS ... OF TRASH!

The Great Pacific Garbage Patch is a huge area of accumulated plastic and trash debris in the North Pacific Ocean, between California and Hawaii. The patch, which is actually two patches (an eastern and western patch) is twice the size of the U.S. state of Texas and estimated to include 1.8 trillion pieces of plastic.

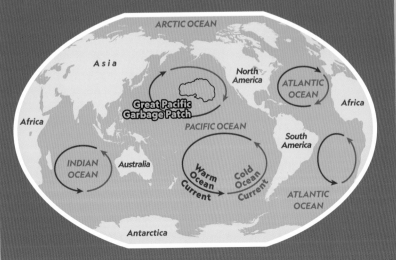

Marine creatures like the sea turtle pictured here can mistake floating bits of plastic (which resemble the jellyfish they eat) for food.

# WHAT ONE WHALE SHOWED US ABOUT EARTH'S PLASTIC PROBLEM

If you want to know just how bad the plastic problem has become in the oceans, just look to the animals that call them home. In November 2019, a sperm whale washed ashore on an island in Scotland with a stomach full of more than 220 pounds (100 kg) of trash and plastic. All the debris in the giant sea creature's stomach had formed a ball that included rope, plastic cups, bags, gloves, packing straps, fishing nets, and tubing. Unfortunately, finding large amounts of trash and plastic inside of sea animals is no longer uncommon. It is yet another reason why it is so important to do our best to use less plastic and to be very careful of how we dispose of garbage.

# MAKE WAVES!

# ORGANIZE A CLEAN, GREEN, TRASH-PICKUP TEAM

Have a free day on the weekend? Grab some friends and family and head to a park or a nearby body of water and—using gloves!—pick up all the trash you can find. Regardless of where plastic litter begins, it can make its way to the ocean. So wherever you are in the world (even if you don't live near a beach!), you can help animals swimming in the great blue seas by reducing litter and plastic pollution.

## 5 SIMPLE WAYS TO USE LESS PLASTIC!

(1) Bring reusable grocery bags with you to the store.

(2) Use a reusable water bottle.

(3) Say "No thanks!" to plastic straws. It is estimated that more than eight billion plastic straws have wound up as pollution on the world's beaches.

(4) Don't throw away your plastic toys. Instead, donate them so they get used again! And when you get to buy a new toy, consider choosing one at a secondhand store rather than a new one all wrapped in plastic!

(5) Taking a trip to the ice-cream shop? Choose a cone instead of a cup and skip the plastic spoon.

## BE AN INSPIRATION!

Consider taking a picture of all the trash you and your team collect. Post it to social media with a parent or guardian's permission or ask your teacher if you can share it with your class. Maybe your great work will inspire others to do the same!

WHEN YOU DO USE **PLASTIC,** MAKE SURE TO DISPOSE OF IT PROPERLY IN A **RECYCLING BIN!**

# PLASTIC POLLUTION WITH A PURPOSE

» One powerful way that artists have found to raise awareness about the plastic that is overwhelming our oceans is by using pieces that have been pulled from the water or picked up from the beach to create eye-opening artwork.

Check out these inspiring artists and how they are bringing attention to the pollution problem lurking in the seas.

## » FROM MENACE TO MASTERPIECE

Artist and art teacher Angela Haseltine Pozzi collects plastic from the beaches near her home in Oregon, U.S.A., which she uses to create giant, eye-catching sculptures. Together with the non-profit she started, Washed Ashore, her team has made more than 80 sculptures out of more than 26 tons (23.5 t) of collected garbage, making seahorses, jellyfish, otters, snakes, sharks, and other animals.

SLEEPING TROLL HILL
DON & JANICE ZERBE
ZACH, ALLIE, ZEPH & EVERETT ZERBE
SATUM, NATE, ELI & LYNA PURDOM

## >>WAVE GOODBYE TO PLASTIC STRAWS

This 11-foot (3.4-m)-tall wave is made from more than 168,000 plastic straws. The artist, photographer Benjamin Von Wong, enlisted a team of hundreds of volunteers to help him collect, clean, and sort the discarded pieces of plastic by color. The piece, titled "Strawpocalypse," also uses collected plastic bags as light diffusers and supports for the straws. The piece illustrates how seemingly little actions, like using plastic straws, can have giant impacts when taken by all the people on Earth.

## >>IT'S GOT A RING TO IT

Made of more than 20,000 pieces of plastic pulled from the ocean, this awe-inspiring arch at the Shanghai Science and Technology Museum stretches some 55 feet (17 m) long. Placed above a mirrored floor, it gives the illusion of a perfect oval. The piece, titled "Giant Ring," aims to bring awareness of the plastic pollution that encircles our planet via our oceans.

**ART** IS A GREAT WAY TO **GET PEOPLE'S ATTENTION, EDUCATE,** AND **INSPIRE!**

# H₂-Oh-Wow!

**Check out this WEIRD BUT TRUE Water Wonder.**

## Great Barrier Reef, AUSTRALIA

Teeming with countless species of marine life, this breath-taking underwater reef is located off the northeastern coast of Australia. All kinds of creatures, from tiny organisms like plankton to gigantic blue whales, call the Great Barrier Reef home. It was built over thousands of years by surprisingly tiny organisms: coral polyps. Coral get their vibrant colors from a microscopic algae called zooxanthellae, which live within the coral in a mutually beneficial relationship. Unfortunately, reefs like this are vulnerable to human impact, through activities such as over-fishing, tourism, and pollution runoff. Coral are also incredibly suscepti-ble to changing ocean temperature, where a simple difference of plus or minus a degree can cause widespread coral bleaching; this is when a stressed coral expels the zooxanthellae, causing it to lose its color and become white. There is hope however: By following some of the tips and suggestions in this book, you'll be doing your part to ensure reefs like this are around for years to come.

CHAPTER

**7**

# WHERE DO WE GO

## *From Here?*

>> **BENJAMIN FRANKLIN SAID, "WHEN THE WELL'S DRY, WE KNOW THE WORTH OF WATER."** Without access to clean freshwater, people cannot survive. If people are drinking contaminated water, traveling miles to collect water, or going without enough to bathe and consume or grow food, it keeps them from being able to fulfill their potential. Not having enough water, or not having clean water, becomes an incredibly challenging barrier for growth and success—both for individuals and for entire communities and countries.

As you take what you've learned out into the world and incorporate new, environmentally friendly habits and behaviors into your day-to-day life, ask yourself:

- *What can I do today to conserve water?*

- *What can I do to keep pollution out of lakes, rivers, streams, and oceans?*

- *How can I reduce my water and carbon footprint?*

- *How can I spread the word about water issues?*

# THREE POWERFUL WAYS TO STAND UP FOR WATER

**W**ater is essential for life. We need it to live, to grow food, to create energy, and for so many other processes that we use in our lives. Water is also a complex issue—there's so much to learn and understand. Hopefully this book has helped you have a better grasp on some of the many different pieces of our planet's water puzzle. You know how much water is on Earth, all the different forms water can take, and some of the challenges facing our planet's water systems and the people who rely on them.

Equipped with this better understanding of all things water, here are three more ways you can advocate for our environment and for people in need around the world.

① **HOLD A FUNDRAISER.** Sometimes one of the best ways to help is to make sure that organizations that are doing great work have the money they need to help more people and do the best job they can. Work with an adult to raise money that you can send to organizations that are inspiring to you. Hold a bake sale or open a lemonade stand, wash neighbors' cars or walk their dogs, or organize a talent show or poetry night with a fee for admission that you'll donate.

② **WRITE OR SPEAK TO YOUR GOVERNMENT LEADERS.** President Barack Obama has often said that the most important role in a civil society is that of a citizen. "It is citizens—ordinary men and women, determined to forge their own future—who throughout history have sparked all the great change and progress," he said. What does that mean? Well, it means that you have a voice and that your voice has power. It means that by speaking up and making your thoughts and ideas heard, you are capable of influencing decisions that are made. It is important, then, that you find ways to express your thoughts, opinions, fears, and passions to the people in your government. Attend town hall meetings, write letters, or visit their office. Be polite, specific, and clear, and make sure to tell them how you hope they will act on the issue that you are discussing.

③ **START A CONVERSATION.** Make sure people know about the issues you care about. Ask your teacher if you can give a presentation to your class or school on a water issue. Talk about what you've learned at the dinner table, create artwork that sparks conversations, or write a poem or an article for your local newspaper.

HOW WILL YOU USE **YOUR VOICE** TO **CREATE** **POSITIVE** **CHANGE?**

# 15 THINGS YOU CAN DO TO BECOME A WATER WARRIOR

1. Find out where the water in your home comes from. What is your water source?

2. Visit a water treatment plant in your community to learn more about the process your local freshwater goes through.

3. Keep a water diary—record how much you use in a day, a week, a month. Brainstorm ways you can cut down on your water usage.

4. Volunteer for an organization that helps people experiencing water scarcity.

5. Encourage your parents and school leaders to have the plumbing in your home and school inspected for leaks.

6. Think about the things you eat, buy, and use. To conserve water, could you adjust your habits so that you waste less food, buy less stuff, and use less energy?

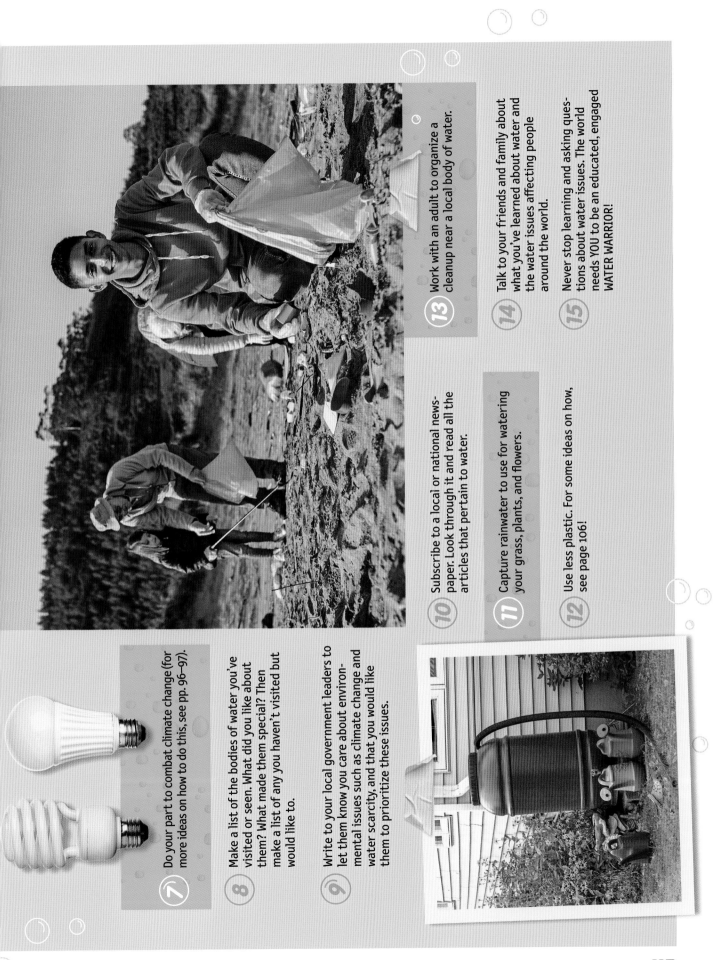

**7** Do your part to combat climate change (for more ideas on how to do this, see pp. 96–97).

**8** Make a list of the bodies of water you've visited or seen. What did you like about them? What made them special? Then make a list of any you haven't visited but would like to.

**9** Write to your local government leaders to let them know you care about environmental issues such as climate change and water scarcity, and that you would like them to prioritize these issues.

**10** Subscribe to a local or national newspaper. Look through it and read all the articles that pertain to water.

**11** Capture rainwater to use for watering your grass, plants, and flowers.

**12** Use less plastic. For some ideas on how, see page 106!

**13** Work with an adult to organize a cleanup near a local body of water.

**14** Talk to your friends and family about what you've learned about water and the water issues affecting people around the world.

**15** Never stop learning and asking questions about water issues. The world needs YOU to be an educated, engaged WATER WARRIOR!

# H₂-Oh-Wow!

**Check out this WEIRD BUT TRUE Water Wonder.**

**Lake Hillier, AUSTRALIA**

When we think of bodies of water, we usually think "blue." But Mother Nature decided to switch things up a bit with this lake! Its incredible cotton candy hue is still a bit of a mystery, but it's thought that it might be due to some combination of three ingredients present in the lake: its high salt content, the red-colored microalgae *Dunaliella salina*, and the pink-colored microbacteria Halobacteria.

## Thanks for reading!

YOU'RE NOW A
**WATER**
WARRIOR!

# An Ode to Water

You catch our breath, so precious and fine.
While neither gold nor diamonds,
You sparkle and shine.

A wily shape-shifter, always on your way to new places,
First frozen, now flowing, then trickling
To hidden underground spaces.

Gush and hammer, drip gentle drops.
You are dazzling,
Whether buried deep in the Earth, or nestled on top.

Whispering secrets from the past that only you could know.
You've swam with whales in the ocean,
Weaved between mountains, been buried deep in the snow.

Thirst you quench, hope you give.
What stories can you tell?
How many lives have you lived?

—Lisa M. Gerry

# INDEX

**Boldface** indicates illustrations.

# PHOTO CREDITS

**COVER** (W lettering), Pineapple studio/Adobe Stock; (A lettering), Pineapple studio/Adobe Stock; (T lettering), Pineapple studio/Adobe Stock; (E lettering), Krafla/Adobe Stock; (R lettering), Krafla/Adobe Stock; (! lettering), Pineapple studio/Adobe Stock; (background), Juri/Adobe Stock; (LE), hadynyah/E+/Getty Images; (CTR), Westend61/Getty Images; (RT), Gary Bell/Oceanwide/Minden Pictures; (water droplets), Kindlena/Shutterstock; back cover (LE), Petr Malyshev/Shutterstock; (RT), Franco Tempesta; (background), alekleks/Adobe Stock; tape pieces (throughout), Picsfive/Shutterstock; water droplets (throughout), Kindlena/Shutterstock; 1, Mike Riley/Getty Images; 3 (W lettering), Pineapple studio/Adobe Stock; 3 (A lettering), Pineapple studio/Adobe Stock; 3 (T lettering), Pineapple studio/Adobe Stock; 3 (E lettering), Krafla/Adobe Stock; 3 (R lettering), Krafla/Adobe Stock; 3 (! lettering), Pineapple studio/Adobe Stock; 3 (background), Juri/Adobe Stock; 4 (UP), Yahya Arhab/EPA/Shutterstock; 4 (CTR), Jake May/The Flint Journal-MLive.com/Associated Press; 4 (LO), Stocktrek Images/National Geographic Image Collection; 5, Richard Thomas/Adobe Stock; 6, Cheryl Zook/NGS; 6–7, wattana/Shutterstock;

**CHAPTER ONE:** 8, Henrik Lehnerer/Shutterstock; 8–9, Tomas Griger/Alamy Stock Photo; 10, Kelsey Smith/Stocksy; 10–11, Dream Lover/Stocksy; 12 (UP), Ivan Gener/Stocksy; 12 (LO), imageBROKER/Adobe Stock; 13 (UP LE), Andrea Bruce/National Geographic Image Collection; 13 (UP RT), Eugene Richards/National Geographic Image Collection; 13 (LO), Jordi Chias/National Geographic Image Collection; 14–15, Chris Philpot; 16 (UP LE), Alexander Chizhenok/Shutterstock; 16 (UP RT), Shannon Hibberd/National Geographic Image Collection; 16 (LO), Jennifer Adler/National Geographic Image Collection; 16–17, Brian J. Skerry/National Geographic Image Collection; 17 (UP), Frans Lanting/National Geographic Image Collection; 17 (CTR LE), Steve Allen/Dreamstime; 17 (CTR RT), Robert Harding Picture Library/National Geographic Image Collection; 17 (LO), David Bowman/National Geographic Image Collection; 18–19, Chris Philpot; 20 (UP), fotomaster/Adobe Stock; 20 (CTR), George Steinmetz/National Geographic Image Collection; 20 (LO), Artens/Shutterstock; 21 (UP), Eyal Bartov/Alamy Stock Photo; 21 (CTR), DedMityay/Adobe Stock; 21 (LO), Alexander Raths/Adobe Stock; 22 (UP), Oleg Senkov/Shutterstock; 22 (LO), OmoniyiAyedun Olubunmi/Alamy Stock Photo; 23 (UP), Gonzalo Ordonez; 23 (LO), Cavan Images/Getty Images; 24, Jennifer Adler/National Geographic Image Collection; 25 (UP), Jennifer Adler; 25 (LO), Jenny Adler/National Geographic Image Collection; 26–27, Gunter Marx/HI/Alamy Stock Photo;

**CHAPTER TWO:** 28, Angela Lumsden/Stocksy; 28–29, Bo Bo/Stocksy; 30 (UP), fashionall/Shutterstock; 30 (LO), Kanstantsin Prymachuk/Dreamstime; 30–31 (background), milo827/Shutterstock; 31 (UP), Preto Perola/Shutterstock; 31 (LO LE), kazoka/Shutterstock; 31 (LO CTR), Africa Studio/Shutterstock; 31 (LO RT), sommai/Adobe Stock; 32 (UP), PhotoGranary/Adobe Stock; 32 (LO), AuntSpray/Shutterstock; 32–33 (UP), Jiayi/Adobe Stock; 32–33 (LO), Dusan Kostic/Adobe Stock; 33 (UP), Andrey Armyagov/Adobe Stock; 33 (CTR), nordroden/Adobe Stock; 33 (LO), Martin D. Vonka/Shutterstock; 34–35, Chris Philpot; 36 (UP LE), Soe Zeya Tun/Alamy Stock Photo; 36 (UP RT), Mariyana M/Shutterstock; 36 (LO), ZUMA Press, Inc./Alamy Stock Photo; 37 (UP), Natalya Danilova/Shutterstock; 37 (LO), Mark Bowler/Alamy Stock Photo; 38 (UP), damircudic/Getty Images; 38 (LO), Capuski/Getty Images; 38 (background), adamkaz/Getty Images; 39, Photononstop RF/Getty Images; 40 (UP), Zoeytoja/Shutterstock; 40 (LO), Elena Schweitzer/Dreamstime; 40–41 (LO), Danny Smythe/Shutterstock; 41 (UP), RTimages/Adobe Stock; 41 (LO), Africa Studio/Shutterstock; 42, Charmaine Chetty; 43 (BOTH), Diane Gouden; 44–45, Stocktrek Images/National Geographic Image Collection; **CHAPTER THREE:** 46–47, hadynyah/Getty Images; 48–49, Michael Hall/Getty Images; 49, Herianus Herianus/EyeEm/Getty Images; 50, rangizzz/Shutterstock; 50–51, Anwa Essop/Associated Press; 51, Wirestock, Inc./Alamy Stock Photo; 52–53, David Mcnew/Reuters; 53 (UP), Mike Blake/Reuters; 53 (LO), Damian Dovarganes/Shutterstock; 54, Rafiq Maqbool/

FOR MY MOM, GAIL; MY SISTER, ALISON; MY BIL, DAN; MY NIECE, ABBY; AND MY NEPHEWS, ANDY AND JACKSON. AND FOR MY DAD, LARRY, A MARINE SCIENTIST AND (IMHO) THE WORLD'S GREATEST WATER WARRIOR. I LOVE YOU ALL. —LMG

Since 1888, the National Geographic Society has funded more than 14,000 research, conservation, education, and storytelling projects around the world. National Geographic Partners distributes a portion of the funds it receives from your purchase to National Geographic Society to support programs including the conservation of animals and their habitats. To learn more, visit natgeo.com/info.

For more information, visit nationalgeographic.com, call 1-877-873-6846, or write to the following address:

National Geographic Partners, LLC
1145 17th Street NW
Washington, DC 20036-4688 U.S.A.

For librarians and teachers: nationalgeographic.com/books/librarians-and-educators

More for kids from National Geographic: natgeokids.com

For rights or permissions inquiries, please contact National Geographic Books Subsidiary Rights: bookrights@natgeo.com

Designed by Brett Challos

The publisher would like to thank the following people for making this book possible: Ariane Szu-Tu, editor; Jen Agresta, project editor; Michelle Harris, researcher; Lori Epstein, photo manager; Gus Tello, designer; the entire Nat Geo Kids Books team; and Sandra Postel, for being the ultimate Water Warrior and inspiration behind this book.

Library of Congress Cataloging-in-Publication Data

Names: Gerry, Lisa, author.
Title: Water! / Lisa Gerry.
Description: Washington, DC : National Geographic Kids, 2023. | Audience: Ages 8-12 | Audience: Grades 4-6
Identifiers: LCCN 2021049834 | ISBN 9781426373558 (paperback) | ISBN 9781426373817 (library binding)
Subjects: LCSH: Water--Juvenile literature.
Classification: LCC GB662.3 .G47 2023 | DDC 553.7--dc23/eng/20211110
LC record available at https://lccn.loc.gov/2021049834

Printed in Hong Kong
22/PPHK/1